Confessions

of a

PASTOR'S
WIFE

New mercies.
Every morning.
Love, Joline

JOLINE PINTO ATKINS

ISBN-13: 978-1537004099
ISBN-10: 1537004093

Find Joline online at:
http://TheCuppaJo.com

Dedication

This book is dedicated to:

George, my beloved partner and teammate, who has always been committed to seeing me flourish—to the extent that he believes it is a huge mistake that I'm not yet famous.

Harper and Zane, who give me plenty of material for my writing binges and hug me because they love me—not because they are "cold" or "tired." Always because they love me. Right?!

Val and Cassie Brkich, who used old-school peer pressure to push me to finish this project so I could sit at a BookFest table with all the other cool kid writers.

Linda Au, who didn't have to agree, but did agree, to tackle turning my blog into this book, due to her incredible support for writers. And crazy people.

Table of Rambling Contents

Foreword
Everybody skips the foreword.
Not you.

I woke this morning glad to see my husband was still home. There was no rush. Sunday School wasn't until ten. I sat in bed with a cup of coffee my son brought me; he had been trained well in the art of bringing a smile to my face by my husband, who has practiced this act of love for years. I didn't even lose my head when he spilled some on the bed. I was excited to attend Sunday School, where we were taking four weeks to address some pretty heated topics: political correctness, the Muslim faith, LGTB issues, and abortion. Truly, who in their right mind would look forward to such a potentially heated morning?

Me.

Because I wasn't rushed. My husband wasn't rushed. My children weren't rushed. We were just normal people waking on the weekend and preparing to head to church.

When my husband first decided to become a pastor, I didn't bat an eye. I knew it was his calling. He'd be great at it. What I wasn't prepared for was that, unlike other professions, I would be linked to his position due to my role as his wife.

Our first candidating experience almost broke my ability to commit to this course in his life, when, after a grueling weekend interview process, word came back that there was concern over hiring George due to the length of my skirts and because, at the time, I was an actress. Except, one glance at my résumé would have revealed my edgy creative endeavors had titles like: *Fiddler on the Roof*, *You're a Good Man, Charlie Brown*, and *Joseph and the Amazing Technicolor Dreamcoat*. Clearly, I was controversial.

And my skirts? It was the '90s. The outfit included opaque tights and a scarf around my neck, reminiscent of a flight attendant's uniform. Their concern gave me pause: who on the search committee was checking out my legs?

For our second church candidating experience, I prevailed. Privy to the game, I chose a Laura Ashley dress and hat for the interview. You want a pastor's wife? I can play a pastor's wife.

Our third attempt at securing a full-time church ministry position would happen in an area outside Chicago, where they understood the arts. The first time I was even invited to the interview process I arrived late, in full stage makeup, having just come from a Sunday matinee.

No one blinked an eye.

We settled in for ten years.

When we felt it was time to move on from our time in Chicago, we turned our sights on western Pennsylvania, putting us closer to family. That interview process, like the last, conveniently and wonderfully placed me as an afterthought, rather than a full-time player in my husband's position. Although I did meet with the elders, I felt incredibly comfortable being me.

We settled in for six more years.

I had never actually been called a pastor's wife in those sixteen years of my life (well, maybe once), but indeed there were situations that gave me pause as to who I was supposed to be in relation to my spouse's place of employment. I had always stood by the mantra that I am a Christian first. A daughter of the King. Who just happens to be the an actress, a mom, a writer, and the wife of a pastor. It wasn't the role or job title that influenced my activity, but rather my position in Christ that served as the filter for my actions.

So, I was surprised when my personal opinions started to become problematic because my husband is a pastor. Perhaps I didn't have a better understanding of the beliefs church members hold about the responsibilities held by a pastor's wife . . . but I couldn't find the standards located in Scripture, either.

The melding of the two—my personal beliefs and opinions with my husband's job title—started feeling claustrophobic.

My identity had never been so wrapped up in someone else's career role.

This inspired me to put pen to paper, or rather, fingertips to keys, as blogging has always cleared my head. And this head was beginning to feel foggy. Who was I in relation to my husband's role?

The *Confessions of a Pastor's Wife* blog series, written over the course of three years, became therapy for me. Those posts, in their original organic state, have been left untouched here, aside from a few minor tweaks and an overall buff and shine.

My beloved husband, George, was even able to remove his pastor's hat and read my words not as a minister, but rather, as my husband, lover, friend, and confidant—enthusiastically offering his thumbs-up support for the project.

He has always been my biggest fan.

Thank you, George. I cannot recall a time during our more than twenty-five years together when you have not supported and celebrated my desire to flourish in my endeavors and dreams.

I wouldn't be a pastor's wife without you.

Wink.

1
Lovely to meet you

We are called to flourish in the life we are given, not in the life we are not given. —Scot McKnight, The Fellowship of Differents

I'm a pastor's wife.

I've been told on *several* occasions that I'm not your "typical" pastor's wife. I do not believe the intent of this statement was meant as judgment—more a reflection of surprise on their part. I don't fit the mold. Which is funny because I'm really not that unconventional. One nose piercing and a weekly margarita fix does not a hipster make.

I can assure you, I am married to a pastor, and thus I am what one would call a pastor's wife.

I'm not exactly sure what makes me atypical, but I can assume this impression comes from the fact that I am:

- **an actress.** At one of George's interviews for his first position, I rushed over to the dinner immediately following the closing number of a show I was in, without stopping to wash off the stage makeup or remove the false eyelashes. I didn't want to be late. And I was hungry. And Evanston "got" the arts, so it really didn't matter.

- **a writer.** I'm outspoken—heck, look at the title of this book!

- **an entrepreneur.** As an actor, writer, former acting coach, and currently a fitness coach, I have designed my own career. As a Beachbody Coach, I post pics of me sweating and flexing and am desperately trying to help others, especially Christians, see that the physical body and one's spiritual walk/growth are so very connected, and that we need to be in good shape to serve Him. Striving to be in strong physical shape is not necessarily vain, and can be an act of worship.

- **not a fan of tradition for the sake of tradition.** I will often challenge "Christianese" and spiritual clichés against theology—*ah, yes, I also went to seminary for a time*—because I dislike empty words. That one was a doozy. "Tell us how you *really* feel, Joline."

- **fiercely independent.** I'm a solution-driven machine. Sometimes my own family can't keep up with me. This can also be a huge problem on the domestic front, but I'm learning how to dial it down and put the whole family *before* my personal goals/desires. So I guess, "fiercely independent" is actually a cover for *selfish*.

And over the next few chapters, I'm going to confess even more thoughts.

But before I do, let's get a few things straight.

- **My heart belongs to Jesus,** not to the church, or to a denomination, or to a ministry.

- **My husband has been called to full-time ministry** and I fully support him.

- **My husband fully supports *me*** and all my wacky and crazy adventures. He is my number-one fan. I cannot think of any instance where he has told me *not* to pursue my creative or professional endeavors.

- **My personal opinion is just that—*my* personal opinion**—and stating it does not mean that I am standing in judgment of opposing opinions. Not even my husband and I agree on everything. WHAT?! Know this: I will tell you what I think. No need for trying to "figure her out." I'm all out. Er, you know what I mean.

So, ready for some confessing?

2
Speechless: Try to keep up with my brain

People can tell you to keep your mouth shut, but that doesn't
stop you from having your own opinion.
—Anne Frank, The Diary of a Young Girl

It's been a while.

I'm alive.

My husband is still a pastor and I am still his wife.

So we've got that going for us.

While I've had a ton of thoughts buzzing around in this noggin of mine, I've been unable to focus on one fully enough to give it star billing for an entire post in my Confessions of a Pastor's Wife series.

But instead of making you wait any longer while I deal with my own A.D.D., I thought it might be fun for you to read a few of the random thought-bytes that I've

18

been juggling. I guess this is what you would call a "post-for-the-sake-of-posting-something-post." At a minimum, this non-post will reveal to you that, even though I've been living caffeine-free (thirty days and counting), my brain *never* stops functioning. Or . . . over-functioning (which may be the truer case).

Disclaimer: Snark alert. And again, think BIGGER PIC-TURE, folks. There is no flaming arrow pointed directly at YOU—as in YOU. Whoever YOU are. Just making observa-tions . . . 'tis all. My musings may be clunky. But they're all mine!

- **Fear is the church's biggest enemy**. Fear of change. Fear of people who are different. Fear of confrontation. Fear of hurting/offending—thus, we avoid hard conversations. I don't hang only in Christian circles, but when I do, I drink Dos Equis . . . (wait, that's not right). When I do, I observe that the most fearful people I know are indeed, people of faith. *(Zing!)* (Side biblical note: The phrase "Fear not" is stated often in the Bible. I've read/heard that it is actually mentioned 365 times. I did not research this. Feel free to do so, and let me know. For me, one "fear not" is good enough to teach me that I should adopt that posture. You don't have to tell me twice!)
- **Christianese is lost on me**. Well, any cliché, really. I cringe at the use of popular phrases and buzz-words, like "hot mess," or, in Christian circles these days, "smokin' hot wife." Really, why are contemporary pastors/writers so attached to that description for their wives? Trying to be hip? Relevant? It's trendy at best. I'm unimpressed. *(Zing!)* It bugs me—

and I'm hot! (Who caught that?) Now, while those two examples don't really scream "Christianese," there are phrases that do fall into this category. And honestly, these phrases create an exclusive subculture that is very uninviting to the people we want to welcome into our churches. Don't believe me? Google "Christianese." Anyway, know that when you utter these phrases, all I hear is Charlie Brown's teacher.

- **There is always a solution.** We cannot foresee the final outcome of tough situations. But, at a minimum, there *are* steps that lead to the final solution available to us. The small steps are progress, if one chooses to see them in that light. It ticks me off when those who claim to have an intense faith cannot see the glimmers of God being present in all things. Even. Just. A. Sliver. Of. Hope. Stop. (Hammer time!) Now, did I just tell folks to stop being pessimists, and in turn, go all-out Pollyanna? Nope. I'd just like to hear, in the midst of doubt and life-crap, an acknowledgment that a solution exists. Maybe not necessarily *the* solution that will remove all the pain and suffering, but even just a tiny celebration: praising God for His presence in the midst of the junk. Hard stuff is hard (how profound). However, knowing that there is a God who reigns over it all, and communicating/living/acting as if that is *true*, are two different approaches to life. Oh, and I've lived this, during the "my-husband-is-depressed-and-can-barely-get-out-of-bed-and-if-he-does-he-cries-in-the-shower-and-thinks-we-would-be-better-off-without-him" years. (As he recently told me when I shared about his depression, "Um, no offense, smokin' hot wife, but my depression was *not* mild. You don't need to downplay it.")

- **Name-it-and-claim-it theology . . . NOT.** Ever.
- **"I'll try to come." "I think I can make it." "Probably."** Are you coming or not? (Okay, this has nothing to do with Christian-anything. It just irritates me.) Well, wait a minute. On second thought, church people, when asked to RSVP for something, please do so. Thanks.
- **Coffee Not-Quite-an Hour**. Anyone wanna take the reins at manning or womanning (personing?) at least *one* table with healthy items during this time on Sunday mornings? Any churches out there do this? Sure, there are donuts. I don't want to mess with tradition. (Well, actually . . .) But, can we not offer something else as well?

(Warned you. Stand up. Stretch. Drink some water. And try to keep up. Because we're moving on.)

- **Temporal or Character-changing Choices?** This is a *huge* question for me these days. I indeed want to journey on the road less traveled, rather than the one that is closest, offers the smoothest terrain, and takes the least amount of effort to navigate. Ah, convenience. How you woo us! No doubt my adventure into the world of health and fitness informs this desire, and yet, there are several spiritual connections to this philosophy as well. I stand firm in my belief that we were given this physical body to serve God. Through observation, I stand firm in my belief that we also neglect the gift of this body, which we were given by God to serve Him and others. We're so caught up on "big sins" that the sin of gluttony (and no, not just with food, but rather with stuff we "need") has been tucked away on the shelf waaaay back in the closet so we don't have to look at it or address it. Guess what? It sees you. That gluttony is coming from inside your house! We are addicted to ease. And I don't know about you, but "easy" is not an adjective I've ever wanted to be called.

- **We may question a lot of things that are happening in this country, such as _____ (insert your own concern), but I'm still thankful I don't live in a theocracy—even though I do love my Jesus.** I really enjoy that, here in America, people have the freedom to believe and live differently than I do. (That includes all the people who may scare you.) (*See first bullet point.*)
- **"God doesn't give us more than we can handle."** False. Please stop saying this.
- **Sin that is hidden/unseen is no less dangerous than sin that we can point to and say, "That's awful!"** That's why it's called sin. It's supposed to be tricky like that. It wants us to believe that one is worse than another. Yet, it all comes from the same root, whether seen or unseen. I know. It sucks. The consequences may be different for different actions, but the root is the same. We blew it. All of us. Both the gossip and the murderer have the same sentence. Thank you, Grace, for saving us both.
- **Everyone is selling something.** Yes, everyone. Even the church. I happen to like what they are handing me, albeit I'm not always a fan of the method in which they do so, but the Ultimate Message? I'm buying. But, don't be fooled, we're all selling something. Everyone. I run from Christian trends: the latest and greatest books, "hip" pastors, packaged products. But church *is* business. Yes, it is. There's

a marketing quality to it. After all, you are reading *this*. So, yeah, I got ya.

- **Gosh darn it, dagnabit, by golly, PLEASE, admit when you need help.** Go to those who have gone before you and ask for advice, read books, *learn always*, dump the pride, and sit under the tutelage (that was fun to type) of someone who knows *more than you* in the area where you need assistance. We have become such an "I can do it myself" society. I have mentors. Women. Men. Those in church. Business. Theater. People to whom I am able to say, "I really don't get this . . . can you help me?" Young marrieds, I'm talking to you also. Grab an older couple and ask that they be a safe place to share struggles. "We never fight." That's ridiculous. Why wouldn't you? George knows *all* of me—even the rough edges—and *that*, my friends, is why our marriage is so stinkin' strong, for we annoy the heck out of each other at times and are still here waiting to take your calls twenty-five years later. Drop the facade. Lower the mask. You're not that good of an actor, anyway. I can tell something's up. Be teachable. Forever.

Random? Yes. I'm well aware. Call this chapter the Ultimate Reset for my Brain. I needed to do a detoxifying dump of my thoughts.

Dumped it on you.

Now maybe I can get back to writing more consistently.

3
Sundays exhaust me

Then Jesus said to them, "The Sabbath was made to meet the needs of people, and not people to meet the requirements of the Sabbath." —Mark 2:27, New Living Translation (NLT)

Sundays wear me out.

And I don't even have any responsibilities on a Sunday morning, other than to get my children up and off to church.

People may wonder why I sit alone at church. Up in the balcony. Not with friends. Not beside other staff members. Just me. In the front pew of the balcony. Sometimes with my son beside me. George joins me for part of the service but has to skip out due to responsibilities after the service. Harper sits in the front pew with her friends.

By choice, and necessity, I worship in my own personal quiet. Because I so rarely am.

Yes, there are people around me. Singing, laughing (our church makes some super-awesome video announcements), and shaking hands (during the "meet someone" part). But, even so, I purposely sequester myself.

Why?

I just need worship to be a rest-stop, rather than a time of fellowship.

I work during the week—just like other people—so, by no means am I claiming weekday martyr status. And even though I work from home, in an office of one, I am in communication with dozens, all day long, and at times, into the evenings. By Friday, like many in a traditional work environment, I'm whooped.

My husband also works during the week (duh), as well as a few nights each week, and is often on call, just due to the nature of being a pastor. Cell phones and texting are a beautiful thing but have also served to blur boundaries a bit. I'm guilty of this myself, so that's not a judgment, just an observation. I hear his phone chirping pretty early. He doesn't have to answer but feels compelled to do so. Back in the days of rotary phones, no one would have thought to call at 5:30 a.m. or after 10:00 p.m. unless it was an emergency. Next week, while on vacation, I'm helping George by making sure his cell phone stays in the hotel room. I think we as a society, both the caller and the receiver, have lost their grasp on what is urgent and what can wait. Immediacy and availability have become our plight. One can always be reached. But should they? Right this second?

Saturday is George's one day off. So, while we'd love to do something fun as a family, we're also catching up on the house or running errands that can't happen during the week. We schedule a few Saturday nights out for the two of us, but the kids want to see Dad. The day itself isn't of the lazy Saturday variety. Often there is a random church something or another on Saturday. For us, that's every other Saturday morning or an event in the evening, There just never seems to be a full Saturday free. If it does happen, it's rare.

And then Sunday comes, and he's back to work, the kids have homework to finish after church that I didn't make them do on Saturday, and I am just craving down time. Quiet time. I spend my weekdays engaged in conversations with people via phone, Facebook, email, and meetings, so there I sit. By myself. In the balcony. Alone. On purpose. To just be quiet. Sometimes I don't even sing. I just listen.

I look down and I pray for the congregation.

I engage with the sermon by taking notes on my Kindle. Evernote and I attend church together. Taking notes is the only way for my brain to stay engaged, and to glean a nugget to take with me into the week.

If I hear a "word" during worship, I immediately note it to be shared with my health and fitness support groups during the week.

There might be lunch out with friends following the service, but sometimes, as was the case last week, during the most beautiful day of the spring thus far, George crashed. Hard. He was in and out of a nap for the remainder of the afternoon because our dogs were barking like crazy due to

CONFESSIONS OF A PASTOR'S WIFE

all the people outside on such a gorgeous day. He missed the beautiful sunshine, and woke from his non-nap without feeling refreshed.

Think I'm whining?

Nope. Just stating. We just don't have a *day*. Or a weekend without responsibility.

Sadly, as a precaution against anyone reading into what I am writing, I feel compelled to add: we are grateful for his job, my job, our home, our friends, etc. We are blessed.

We're just a bit wiped out. Other than vacation, once or twice a year, we haven't experienced the typical weekend in fifteen years. Pastors don't really seem to have a complete day off.

So if I seem quiet on a Sunday morning, or uninterested in engaging in conversation, or if I don't linger for chit-chat, it's not you. Ha ha, I just gave you the "It's not you, it's me" line.

And if it sounds as if Sundays hit me hard, you should see my Monday . . .

4
I'm not actually on the payroll

A gossip betrays a confidence; so avoid anyone who talks too much. —Proverbs 20:19, New International Version (NIV)

I guess the title of this chapter does come across a bit cheeky.

Consider it to be truth, wrapped in a tease.

Truth: My *husband* is on the payroll, not me.

Tease: I don't confess this because I'm embittered in any way and feel I need to be paid for services rendered. That couldn't be further from the truth.

Here's what troubles me. In my fifteen years of being married to a pastor, I've lost count of the number of times I have had a conversation with a church member that goes something like this:

"I met with George today."

"Cool."

"He didn't tell you?"

"Nope."

"So he didn't tell you what I shared with him?"

"Absolutely not!"

Sounding confused, "Oh, but I just figured he shared that kind of stuff with you."

"Oh no, what church members share with George doesn't come home. If he feels that my perspective can be helpful, he asks permission to share with me. But as a general rule, no, I don't need to know what is discussed."

"I had no idea."

I'm always baffled by this. Just like a doctor or therapist, the information shared in private meetings George has with church members should not become dinner discussion. And I'm surprised that someone would assume this happens. *And* would be okay with it. Anyone reading this who may have assumed that 1) pastors share your personal information with their spouses, and that 2) this is acceptable behavior, should know that it is not okay for your personal information to be shared with the wife of the pastor, unless express permission has been given. You should feel confident that your pastor is not bringing his work home.

See, George is the only one in our household paid by the church to counsel church members. To offer confidential counsel. I am not. Although I do meet with members also, I usually do so over coffee. Or with a margarita. Or hunched over while getting my nose pierced.

It's . . . different.

Not being an actual staff member has its perks. For every so often I choose to opt-out of a Sunday, because, well . . . I'm tired. I also don't make it to every event. And while I've served in women's ministry and directed our Christmas production of *Let It Be Christmas*, I am careful to pray and discern where God has called me to serve, rather than agreeing to participate in anything I'm asked, simply because I am married to a staff member. And often that place of service is not directly by my husband's side. GASP! I'm still his partner in ministry; I just don't necessarily take his classes. Nor did he co-direct the musical. Although I did let him paint a "No Vacancy" sign.

I'm currently waiting on God's call for where I should serve next. The magic 8-ball seems to be stuck on "Reply Hazy."

Thankfully, I don't have a job description to follow, or hours to log, so I'll wait patiently on the answer.

Consider it a non-paid leave of absence.

Oh, wait . . . I'm not actually on the payroll.

5
I flunked Beth Moore

*Good spiritual directors understand that people have
different spiritual temperaments, that what feeds one doesn't
feed all. Giving the same spiritual prescription to every
struggling Christian is no less irresponsible than a doctor
prescribing penicillin to every patient.*
—Gary L. Thomas, Sacred Pathways: Discover Your
Soul's Path to God

I tried. I really tried.

Raise your hand if you've ever participated in, and completed, a Beth Moore study. She knows her stuff. As in, *really* knows her stuff. So, it would stand to reason that I would eat it up. The details. The knowledge. The organization of it all. Beth Moore's Bible studies are tight. They are packaged well. The content is solid. The teaching is top notch.

Didn't matter.

I flunked out.

I began a study with a few girlfriends in the fall. We would watch the video one week, do the workbook homework on our own during the week, and then return the following week to discuss it. I was doing well for a few months, even though my interest was waning. As I'd made a commitment to my friends, I tried to keep up. I couldn't put my finger on why it wasn't clicking for me. But clearly, it wasn't. Still, I'd watch the video lesson, take notes, and do my homework during the week. Only, I started to get lazy. I'd end up doing three days of homework in one sitting. Those who have done a Beth Moore study know that cramming simply isn't possible. The content is too detailed and there's a lot of it. Shoving it all together in one sitting is pointless. I began to resent the workbook and had no desire to crack it open. My focus toward reading and answering the questions slowly dwindled, and finally, by the new year, I had to admit to myself, and to my friends, that . . .

Okay, here it comes . . .

I'm just not that into Beth Moore.

And I desperately wanted to be.

There! I said it. (Wow, talk about breaking free.)

Is this a criticism of Beth Moore? Absolutely not! Is this a lesson in personal learning styles? Absolutely.

I read. I write about what I read. And this year I've tackled a 30-day devotional called *Soul Detox*, am currently enjoying a daily devotional with excerpts from the writings of C.S. Lewis, and I couldn't get enough of *Every Body Matters: Strengthening Your Body to Strengthen Your Soul* by Gary

Thomas. I have found comfort in Anne Lamott's *Thanks, Help, Wow,* and am just about to crack open *The Emotionally Healthy Church* by Peter Scazzero, at the persistent, yet gentle nudging of my husband. I keep a one-line journal, a daily diary in which I limit myself to penning one sentence, the outcome of which often feels like a sputtered, albeit incredibly honest prayer. (I know, I know, I'm wordy. It seems inconceivable that I would ever be able to keep a journal entry to one sentence.) I spend my days in silence, for the most part, other than a few phone calls to customers during the day, and I am thankful to have time to commune with God and read throughout my day since I work from home.

What I find hilarious is how a person like me, who has a timer go off every night to remind me to write my to-do list for the next day, and who follows a workout calendar like it's the boss, could not develop the discipline of doing my Beth Moore homework every day. She's a strong teacher and knows her Bible—and I dig that—but the study itself? Not for me.

Did I mention I tried?

• Perhaps the issue was with the workbook-style teaching.

• Perhaps because I am pretty tightly scheduled during my day, I need more of the free-style that I can get from books, rather than the routine of a fill-in-the-blank.

• Perhaps the answer is simpler. And I'm just not that into Beth Moore.

One would think I would be. She's funny. She's got great delivery. She's passionate. She knows her content. She's entertaining, direct, and tells a great story.

Light bulb.

At the risk of sounding like I'm feeding myself compliments here, perhaps we are just too much alike? My personality can be a bit much—even for me—so perhaps I gravitate toward my opposite?

Or, I could be overthinking this whole thing, and just need to be okay with saying that, while Beth Moore is a crazy amazing teacher, she's just not my cup of coffee.

WARNING! The first person who turns around and misquotes/twists my words about not digging the studies and shares shock that I wrote about how I don't like/am critical of Beth Moore herself?

You're gonna get punched.

6
I have no idea where to sit at the potluck

Pass the damn ham, please.
—Harper Lee, To Kill a Mockingbird

Get in line. Careful with the choices: this is a potluck. One can sabotage an entire week of hard work just from one pass through the church potluck line. There are lots of offerings with mayo, cream, or melted cheese. The dessert table is longer than the actual real food table. Always choose salad. Fruit. Save room for that roasted pig. Not too heavy on the chips. Help the kids get their hot dogs, hamburgers, or . . . roasted pig.

Get a drink.

Find a seat.

Hmmm, that's the tricky part.

Wander a bit.

Wander some more.

I never know where to sit at these things.

Next to George? Nope, he's not sitting. He's working.

With the kids? Nope, they are with other kids.

The worship pastor's wife? Always a safe bet. She's family.

But, the nagging question emerges: Shouldn't I be meeting new people? Branching out?

This happens to me at most large meal events at church. I have no idea where to park myself. Usually, as is the case during Sunday morning Coffee Not-Quite-an Hour, I look for new faces, ones I've not met, or ones that seem like they too do not know where to sit, and I join them. Other times I hook up with the small group of people I have come to know well. But when I do this, I feel as if I'm not doing my "job."

Which, is odd, because I don't actually work at the church.

More often than not, I have learned that if I don't approach a group, I will most likely sit with one person, sit alone, or position myself right on the outskirts of a group. Which often results in my choosing to flit from table to table. I remember our first week at our new church. We had just been introduced to the congregation, and yet there I was awkwardly walking around at a picnic following the service, introducing myself to people because no one was approaching me.

This is not meant to sound whiny or woe-is-me-y, it's just an observation.

I'm a pocket-watcher. We like our social pockets. Even

in a small congregation, we have them. People sit in the same spot in church. Down in Coffee Not-Quite-an Hour, the same groups congregate from week to week. At church dinners? Same deal. *Myself included*. There is nothing wrong with this, unless:

- One is a staff person's wife whose husband is responsible for people making connections in our congregation. Then, there's an unspoken expectation (which I've created) telling me that I must do so as well. There's a bit of truth to this, for I have received comments like, "People don't know you." So, I need to approach them.

- One is new to the church. Often, even after living here for four years, I still feel new. Many folks who live in the area have a long history with each other. I'm a transplant. And still feel like one.

Church potlucks are interesting. On one hand, I'm so excited that I don't have to spend money eating out or go home to make lunch because, as I've already shared, Sundays are tiring. On the other hand (and, don't worry, there are only two hands), they create self-induced stress, mainly due to my own internal pressure to make sure that I am being friendly, or because I feel like I'm interfering with a group and am not sure of my place.

Surprised? Even just a little bit?

Well, this is called *Confessions of a Pastor's Wife* and it would be rather rude if I teased you with that title and then didn't deliver.

It's true.

I really have no idea where to sit at the potluck . . .

But I am always hungry, so I'll see you there!

7
Come on over, but bring your own napkins

Real freedom is freedom from the opinions of others. Above all, freedom from your opinions about yourself.
—Brennan Manning, The Wisdom of Tenderness: What Happens When God's Fierce Mercy Transforms Our Lives

I suck at hospitality.

At our last church, I was amazed by our senior pastor's wife, who was also the director of worship, because whether it was Christmas, Easter, or just some random Sunday on the church calendar, she was always set for guests. Even though she and her husband were working full-time at our church.

The house was always clean.

The table was always set.

The food was always delicious.

And it seemed like she could handle a steady stream of visitors without a hitch.

This. Is. Not. Me.

I have friends who do this well.

But me? I never seem to have enough glasses. Or plates. I've had to borrow extra spoons from other friends. Ample supply of serving dishes? Forget about it. Plus, our table just doesn't fit people comfortably. It's not that I have this Downton Abbey complex—that I need to be able to pull off a formal gathering—but my casual gatherings don't seem to cut it, either. In my opinion.

And embarrassingly, we've often had people over for dinner and not even had napkins available. We joke about the "community hand towel," but truly, this is how it has gone down at times when we've had people over for dinner. It's either that, or I pull out the napkins my Nanny embroidered for me—which would work, only I just now thought of it as a solution. See? My mind doesn't do hospitality well.

I know, I know, "It doesn't have to be perfect!" (I'm not sure I totally believe—that all people really believe—this often-quoted sentiment. Paranoia much?)

I've been told that the house doesn't have to be perfectly clean and the table perfectly set, but unfortunately, I really want these two things to be in place when I have guests, so if we can't get it together, I'd rather not do so. Thus, I don't extend invitations as often as I would like.

Plus, there are the dogs. That's a whole other chapter.

Once again, as I mentioned during my potluck chapter, much of my concern over what people may think is completely self-induced, and I'm sure that many couldn't care less how my house looks. Or how the table is set. Admittedly, I have had a few "You've never had me over for dinner" comments, which is just awkward, because my failure to invite seems to reflect my lack of interest in the party involved, rather than the truth of my own insecurity about pulling off dinners the way I would love to pull off dinners. I do see how this could be perceived as a slight.

Thus, I'm confessing. It's not you. It's me.

Recently, I came across the perfect statement on Facebook, and I think I ought to adopt it as a personal mantra:

"Dull women have immaculate houses."

I've rarely been called dull. Usually I'm called other choice words, which I'd be glad to chat with you about over a meal.

Somewhere other than my house.

8

There ought to be a seminary course for future pastors' wives

*I never realized until lately that women were supposed to be
the inferior sex.* —Katherine Hepburn

This chapter risks offending a few people.

Ah, heck, what else is new?

While at seminary, there was a special award given
to the wives of seminary students upon their husbands'
graduation: the "PHT" certificate.

PHT = Putting Honey Through.

George obviously knew me well enough not to submit
my name to receive this certificate. I'm sure many couples
found it cute. It disturbed me.

During those seminary years, I first served as the execu-
tive office coordinator for the academic dean of the college
connected to the divinity school. Two years into George's

graduate program, I moved to the Campus Ministries Department, coordinating that office, activities, and staff, along with the worship teams for our chapel services. By the time he had graduated and started job hunting, I had advanced to becoming the director of campus ministries. Yes, my salary and the generous employee tuition cut certainly helped in "putting honey through," but I also used those years to advance my own career as he was studying to advance his. So, I never felt like our time there was all about *his* degree, but rather, our mutual growth. Along with my job at Trinity College, I was also a seminary student myself, serving as an adjunct professor, directing two musicals at the college, and I found a steady freelance gig directing the musicals at a nearby elementary school for several years. It was a super-busy time.

I never once saw my role as "putting honey through." We simply had jobs and responsibilities and helped each other to embrace and complete them well.

I recall attending a luncheon with Henry Blackaby, author of *Experiencing God*, while at seminary. It was a luncheon in the middle of my work day, and I was dismayed to show up to find that my name tag read "Mrs. George Atkins" rather than "Joline Pinto Atkins—Director of Campus Ministries," when all the the other male directors who were invited had their titles on their tags. Am I being silly? I think not. Not only was I taking a team of students through Mr. Blackaby's book, but my husband, who also attended the luncheon as the coordinator of discipleship ministries, worked for me.

Yes, he reported to me.

Anyway, that gives you a little background into why "putting honey through" just made me cringe.

Why is the "PHT" and my time as a staff member at seminary even relevant?

Because now, twenty years into ministry, that "PHT" award seems to stand out as a firm reminder to me that I believe there is a hole in seminary education, that hole being 1) a class for the husband about his wife's role (or non-role) in his future ministry; and 2) a class for the wife outlining the truths of being a pastor's wife, Pastor's Wife-isdom 501. And since there are women getting their divinity degrees, perhaps it is the *husband* who needs a bit of a syllabus outlining what the professional years will bring about as the spouse of a pastor.

So naturally, my mind initially returned to my time at seminary when a friend recently sent me a blog post entitled "Seven Things Pastors' Wives Wished They'd Been Warned About." If only there had been a comprehensive course on this very subject for both the spouses of seminarians as well as our future pastors. It would have been great to have a seasoned pastor's wife share with me that it is okay to be myself behind church doors. The "me" that includes performer, wellness coach, acting coach, and friend—hanging with my closest friends . . . at a bar.

Kidding.

Hiccup.

9
I'm considering homeschooling, but not for the reason you may think

Everything is art. Because everything has been designed.
—Zane Everett Atkins, age 7

Homeschooling.

It's not just for conservative Christian families any longer.

That's a stereotype, one that I used to believe myself. Simply because those were the only people I knew who did so. I've learned my lesson.

I now know several families who have chosen to teach their children at home, with a traditional homeschool method, or via cyber school. And for several, their decision to do so is not solely based on religious convictions.

I am a product of public school, as is my family. My husband. His family. My children have been in public school since preschool. The snapshot memories I have of school are positive ones. For some odd reason I remember most vividly a report I wrote about Monticello in fourth grade, ending my essay with a very dramatic, "And then, it burnt to a crisp!" It would seem that I began my habit for adding literary "jazz hands" to my pieces at a very young age.

While I do harbor some concerns about public school education, I am not researching the homeschooling option out of anger or elitism. When someone asks me why, my answer, albeit perhaps naive or juvenile, is "Because I think my kid needs more."

More what?

Zane is an independent learner. A reader. He starts and finishes homework without prodding. He enjoys projects. And he is very inquisitive. The questions he asks me on a Sunday drive to church are philosophical in nature, and, at times, over my head. (Wait? So how could I teach him? Oh no . . .) Am I saying he's a genius?

Heck no.

But, lately, he has begun communicating boredom. In his gentle, old-soul way, he has shared that at times it's hard to complete work with a partner in class because the talking is distracting. I know for a fact that he is not innocent of being a distraction himself. It's not as if I'm saying my precious snowflake can do no wrong. He mentioned this week that he needed to position himself at a table by himself at school so he could finish his Haiku and Sanguine poems away from other kids who were talking. Again, there were no dramatic emotions infused into these statements. But they did give me pause. You see, he really enjoys learning.

And while this may sound horribly judgmental, here it is:

Public school does come with soooooooooooo much other stuff. (Okay, life does, too. I hear you. But, this is my story, yo.) And as I watch my eight-year-old crave information (he keeps a question notebook), I am concerned that this hunger he has is at risk of flat-lining.

There. I said it. *Beep. Beep. Beep. Beeeeeeeeeeeeeeeeeeeeeeeeeee eeeeeeeeeeeeeeeeeeeeeeeeeeeeeeeep.*

Amidst social pressures and hours of homework (worksheet after worksheet after worksheet), and the fatigue of an 8–4 day (taking into account the thirty-minute bus ride he would have to and from school upon hitting third grade), I foresee a "dulling down" effect. That's what my "mother gut" is telling me. It makes me want to initiate educational CPR. Yet, there is an alternative. He could be learning more information in half that time, as well as choosing some elective classes in areas of interest, such as photography and art, via the homeschool or cyber route.

The majority of learning would happen with me, but my research has shown that there are several options for group connection with other homeschooled children in the area. The beauty of what I do for a living is that I can work virtually anywhere. Literally, virtually: from laptop, smartphone, tablet. So, although I would now have to establish concrete "store hours," which I've needed to do anyway, I am not tied down by having to run to/from a brick-and-mortar location every day.

As for Harper? We are exploring a performing arts charter school for her (in graphic art) which, while public, operates on block scheduling (which is better for the way she thinks/organizes) and would give her the opportunity to explore her interests as part of the daily curriculum. If she is not accepted to the school, I'm not sure what we will do . . .

So, is this post about the public school? No.

Is this post about *you* choosing public school? No.

Have I made any disparaging comments about the state of public education? No.

Is it sad that I have to explain myself? Yes.

Do I think my son would excel in a homeschooling model? Yes.

The thought of homeschooling has been lingering with me for years. I never researched it thoroughly because 1) I didn't think I had the brains to do it; 2) upon moving to western Pennsylvania we had some big-time adjusting to do as a family; 3) I started a new business three years ago that I needed the time to build while the kids were in school; 4) I had this misunderstanding that if you homeschooled, you did so for life (now I realize we can reevaluate from year to year); and 5) I didn't know where to start.

Reasons why I now think I'm ready?

Because I think my son needs it and would benefit from it.

And if that's the case? I accept.

10

So, about that plate of cookies you sent home with my husband . . .

Everything in moderation, including moderation.
—Oscar Wilde

I threw it out.

Disclaimer: This confession spans more than fifteen years of ministry. So, if you think this post is about you, I'd like to introduce you to a song by Carly Simon.

A chat with a fellow pastor's wife over a cuppa tea this week reminded me that I needed to unload this confession. It went down something like this.

"Alice, share with me one of your pastor's wife confessions."

"I'm tired of my home being the dumping ground for all the food that is brought to the church!"

48

YESSSSSSSSSSSSSSSSSSS!

My friend, along with her husband (the pastor—you keeping up?), happen to be in one of my health and fitness groups and they are working so very hard on developing the habit of daily exercise and revamping their nutrition. They both have weight-loss goals and have placed themselves in my accountability group to do so.

And yet, there is the cake.

Cookies.

Cupcakes.

(Okay, so not ALL of it is dessert-y, but the majority of it is.)

Plates of food. Gone uneaten.

Offered to them. Out of the blue. After church events. "Or it will go to waste!" (How 'bout not making so much food to begin with? But that's for another chapter.)

Food has become such a go-to gift.

And a curse.

"If something is left-over, they just send it home with [insert her husband's name]. Even if he says 'no thanks.' Home it comes. And we dump it. I feel awful for dumping, but we don't want it. And we feel like we have to take it."

This scenario just smells of people taking things too personally.

When we offer something, like a plate of brownies, if the receiver says, "No thanks," let's not take that so personally. Take my house, for instance. We just don't have that stuff around the house. Why? Because while George and I are disciplined, we're also crazed, obsessed fanatics. . . . We just *know ourselves*. We would eat the entire plate. I've been known to eat an entire bag of chocolate chips in one sitting. *We know our weaknesses.* Which is why we choose discipline. Which is why we say, "No, thank you." It's not a reflection on the giver; it's a reflection of our personal weakness.

Years ago, in another congregation, my husband told the staff outright that his doctor asked him to lower his weight and cholesterol. He asked the staff for help by not bringing in dessert for staff meetings, or to at least have a healthy alternative available.

Deaf ears. Donuts. Bagels. Cream cheese. Nary a fruit to be found. After the meeting the food would remain in the staff office area, beckoning each passerby with that "come hither" look.

Yes, yes, I realize that people like to show their gratitude, and yet, in church settings, it just seems that 75% of the time, gratitude is shown via the stomach.

I can tell you what a pastor *would* appreciate.

A thank-you note.

Tickets to the movies. (Or a night out with his spouse.)

Fresh veggies from your garden.

But donuts? Or leftovers from that ministry meeting?

We appreciate the sentiment, but sorry, Charlie, we're not bringing it home. Either someone else will eat it, or it will get thrown away.

Which is exactly what you didn't want to happen.

And yet, it just did.

(We love that you want to feed us. It's sweet. Only, hear us. I have my husband on a vegetarian diet to help lower his cholesterol and keep him off medication, and my friend who offered the confession for this post has some big weight-loss goals herself, as does her husband. Support us in these goals and keep your pastors healthy!)

You'll be happy to know I didn't throw out the dish on which the cookies came.

I just can't find it.

11
My children are not "PKs"

And so it was, that Jesus died on the cross. Between two feet.
—Harper Ella Atkins, age 3

I first heard the term "PK" when I worked at Trinity College outside of Chicago.

I had no idea what it meant.

When someone explained it, my initial thought was, "Wow, that's some kind of awful pressure to put on a kid."

Later, my pastor–husband and I had children . . .

My children wear mismatched clothes, ripped jeans, and ski-caps to church. They don't always memorize the verses for Sunday school, or complete the devotionals that are sent home. They fidget in the pew and get bored. They will not pray out loud. Sometimes during the music part of worship they remain seated rather than standing with everyone else.

I've asked my daughter why she sits during singing. Her answer was quite clear.

"I just like to watch and listen." And, I get that. There are times when the entire congregation can be standing in unison, but I feel compelled to stay seated. So I do.

Only, I know there is another reason behind her answer.

I remember years ago, when my daughter was four, she began to get very shy in church. As in, phobic shy. And I use that word clinically, not mom-otionally. (I made that word up.)

When I asked her what made her so nervous, she responded with, "Everyone is watching me."

What?

Around that same time, after the Youth Sunday service, an older church member approached Harper (rather than me) and proceeded to tell her that she had been a distraction during the service. I stepped in. Oh, yes, I did.

"Ma'am, it is Youth Sunday, and I happen to lead a small group of many of those youth leading worship today. They also babysit my daughter, and they invited her to sit up on the platform during worship."

It didn't help.

Anyway, it was during that particular year that Harper seemed to catch on that because Daddy was a pastor, and because she was his kid, many people, most of whom she didn't even know, sure knew who she was. Imagine being four and having a bunch of strangers calling you by name and making comments—even well-meaning ones—every Sunday.

"You sat so nicely."

"I saw you put money in the offering plate."

"You seemed to enjoy the children's sermon."

"I love what you are wearing."

And, of course, the "You were very distracting today."

For some children, this would be a sign to them that they are being watched. She caught on that she was visible. And didn't like it. At all.

It was that year that she decided not to sit up front for the children's sermon any longer and got super nervous in vacation Bible school and wouldn't participate. And something as simple as attending Sunday school became a chore.

I'm not saying that being watched was the cause of this newfound social anxiety within her, but I do believe that it added to some of the extreme shyness that began to surface.

I resolved during those early years, and based on what I was seeing with her, that I would not put "Pastor's Kid" pressure on either of my children. They could dress how they wanted and sit where they wanted, as long as they were respectful, which we have had to address from time to time. Don't turn around and comment that my kids should be well-behaved in church, because I have been that mom who whisks my child up and removes them from the service. I've also told them they could be involved in whatever they would like at church—as much or as little—as long as they were involved in some way. There has never been "You should know better! Daddy is the associate pastor!" talk around this house. That would be downright cruel.

And I don't think people are watching my children that closely, really (I hope), but even the joking murmurings of "PK" bugged me due to the story I just unfolded.

I think we all agree that labeling is uncool.

Pastors' kids do not have to be straight arrows. Nor do they turn out to be hell-mongers. They are children. We don't hear the term "CEO's Kid," or "Doctor's Kid," or "Sanitation Driver's Kid."

We may not realize that even little ears are listening. And our words penetrate. Deeply.

Meet my children. Harper and Zane.

Their father just so happens to be a pastor.

12
Dirty mouth? Try Orbit!

I love Jesus, but I cuss a little. —Unknown

I'm not *that* bad.

I don't let the F-bombs fly (well, not as a regular habit), and I try hard not to even utter its brother-from-another-mother, *friggin, freakin* or *phat*. (And really. Fess up, for when you use those words, we all know you are merely substituting them for the mac-daddy F-word, which albeit inaudible, is still in your thoughts. You're not fooling anyone.)

However, I have been known to let an *a-word* and a few *sh-words* escape. Okay, so there's also the *H–E–double hockey sticks* and *crap*, which is just another word for that *sh-one*. I'm hopeless. I've cleaned it up here. But let's be honest.

I cuss.

I'm not a sailor. But I can play one on TV.

I can't stand foul language as a rule. It's lazy language. Even in theater/film, I really wish they would come up with something more descriptive to say. I have only had to let 'er rip once during a show I did in Pittsburgh. But the monologue totally called for it, so I gave it all I had.

And yet, I can be salty. For the church folk.

Case in point: Sunday. In the course of a ten-minute conversation, I joked about someone going to the woods behind the church to smoke weed and asked our children's pastor if he had just used the word "whore" in a sentence.

And while the dialogue didn't include any customary cursed concoctions, and was incredibly mild for the world, the casual use of "weed" and "whore" in general conversation would have raised an eyebrow in certain company. It had my husband doing that thing he does where he shakes his head and says, "And you wanna be a pastor's wife," reminiscent of Seinfeld to George Costanza, "And you wanna be my latex salesman!"

I guess this is a true confession about my personal issues with the tongue, rather than my usual commentary on Pastor's Wife-ism.

Thought I should tell you.

Nothing a little Lifebuoy can't cure, right? Worked for Ralphie.

13
Things I've done to make a quick buck

We get one story, you and I, and one story alone. God has established the elements, the setting and the climax and resolution. It would be a crime not to venture out, wouldn't it? —Donald Miller, Through Painted Deserts

Made you look.

Last time on *Confessions of a Pastor's Wife* I confessed my sailor-speak. How about we continue getting to know each other? I'll start. It's my book.

My husband spent four years in seminary, during which, rather than sit home alone while he studied Greek (a year of Greek in six weeks, or "Suicide Greek" as it was *affectionately* known), I decided to hit the stage again.

A local community theater was doing *Hello, Dolly!* I was the third person to audition. The director, who became a very valued friend in my life, said she cast me within thirty seconds of my opening my mouth. While my husband studied in his closet of an office with an old door for a desk and the original Mac, I spent nights at rehearsals. Having a blast.

Having not performed since high school, I knew that it was time to continue pursuing this long-forgotten area of my life.

I had a full-time job at the time, working for both the academic dean of Trinity College and as an adjunct professor directing shows such as *Joseph and the Amazing Technicolor Dreamcoat* and *The Fantasticks*. I also directed shows at a nearby elementary school. I finished my tenure at Trinity as the director of campus ministries.

Following George's graduation with his master's of divinity, I made the *brilliant* move to quit my full-time job to become an actress. Ah, youth. And so began my search for any job, within reason, that would pay me. Preferably in cash.

George held down his job managing Newport Coffeehouse, while also valet parking at an Italian restaurant that was rumored to be connected to the Mob (no joke), painting in people's homes, mowing lawns, and ... I'm sure there was more. We lived on house-sitting gigs, in massive homes where we threw Oscar parties and even a fantastic Easter dinner when we called the family while they were on vacation to ask whether they kept kosher—because you know we Christian folk love our ham. Yes, we were, and still are, sensitive like that. We grilled their steaks and swam in their pools, and frowned at rooms filled with leather-bound books that were obviously just for show, as evidenced by the creaking they made when opened.

Then there was me. The actress.

My legit job was teaching for a local children's theater company. Then, upon auditioning for a professional company, the artistic director pulled me aside and said, "You are both too young for a part, and too old for another, but would you like to teach for us?" This was *the* premier place to teach—and thus, I left the other company and began my ten years as an instructor with Apple Tree Theater. But, I still needed to bring in more.

Enter . . . ANYTHING.

Cap'n Crunch, anyone? There was the time my agent called and said, "Wanna make eighty dollars?" Um, yes. And that's exactly what I was paid after spending a hot August afternoon in the worst—no kidding—most dangerous part of Chicago trapped inside a blow-up Cap'n Crunch costume, complete with my own air pump. I had to be walked around the park so I wouldn't trip, while my "handlers" passed out boxes of Cap'n Crunch. I got paid the $80 and a huge box of trial size boxes of Cap'n Crunch.

Will work for pie. I also performed in Murder Mystery Parties. Correction, *1920s flapper* murder mystery parties. Fifty bucks a show. And, an apple pie. This was treacherous terrain, for all the guests ended up getting drunk, and several times I ended up on some old guy's lap, to which I'd add in my best New York accent, "Hands off, Mista!" Oh, did I mention that my character was the murderer? Score. Between the old drunk guys and the murder, I should have received a second pie.

Knock your socks off! If you can find a copy of this commercial for a K-Tel record collection of songs from the 1950s, I will seriously give you something for your time. Imagine someone's home and a bunch of hard-up actors in '50s garb, dancing all afternoon. I think I maybe broke $100. (Note, once I went SAG, the jobs got way better.)

Broadway Blend. Tips, please! One of my favorite gigs was a Broadway revue that I did with two theater buddies at Newport Coffeehouse. We packed the place. And worked solely for tips. The outcome was so good that each of us walked away with about $100 for two hours of singing. My favorite number? The one I sang with my friend Danny—"Barcelona"—which is all about a one-night stand. And you wanna be a pastor's wife . . .

I wasn't in *Friends*, but I worked with a guy who was. Extra work. Not great money. Tons of sitting-around time. But, kind of fun. I did extra work on *My Best Friend's Wedding*, *Miracle on 34th Street* (clinched a close-up in that one), and this movie directed by *Friends* star David Schwimmer. Not only will you find me dancing (which George and I were surprised to see when it aired one night while he was interviewing for a church position in New York), but I'm also on the back of the video box. Well, barely. But I'd know that hair anywhere. I don't remember what I was paid for any of these extra gigs. Enough to pay a few bills. But not enough to pay rent, I'm sure.

I wasn't an actor who waited tables. I was all data entry. Friends of ours owned a company where they worked with lighting companies all over the United States. I entered the stock. For $10 an hour. I fit this in between auditions and teaching.

Happy birthday to many, many, many children. At some point, and I really don't know how this happened, I started booking myself at birthday parties. For $125, I could be booked to do a dance party or an acting class party. These were hot. Very hot. Later, when I took up the ukulele (yup) and the guitar, I did music and movement parties for the toddler set. I was known as "Jojo, the Music Mama." It's all true. Every word.

"Sing out, Louise!" I started privately coaching promising young hopefuls for theatrical and on-camera auditions when a child's mother called and asked if I could choreograph "Swanee" for her then-five-year-old who would be performing it in a talent show. I charged $35 an hour. That boy is now in his twenties and one of my favorite performers to date. Even now, I get choked up thinking of all the auditions we prepped for over the years. By the time I left Chicago, I was asking—and getting without any question—$100 an hour, mainly because of his family, who referred me to everyone who was anyone. They threw a going-away party for me before we moved to Pittsburgh, during which my most regular students sang to me a song written by this first student. He also sang "Swanee" at that party. Tears. Lots of tears.

As the years progressed, the acting jobs got much better, thanks to my union card, an amazing agent, and a national commercial for Coldwell Banker. As I look back, I am thankful for all my experiences. The corporate industrial films, where I was always cast as a Hispanic, the small theaters that paid me even a meager amount, and even that creepy audition in the back of a bar where a friend and I had to act as private detectives (Charlie's Angels style) for a film that was apparently going to be filmed in the Bahamas. (We slipped out a back door . . .)

Why even share this?

I was recently discussing it with my trainer at Beachbody Corporate—all I used to do to make ends meet. And I'm sure I've forgotten a few gigs. We didn't have Facebook or Instagram or even digital photography to record them. So, you'll have to envision me in that Cap'n Crunch get-up.

All I know is that I did what I had to do. And kept it clean. (With one—only *one*—showgirl costume.)

Love,

Your Pastor's Wife

14
Lest you think I don't have bad habits

With habits, we don't make decisions, we don't use self-control, we just do the thing we want ourselves to do—or that we don't want to do. —Gretchen Rubin, Better Than Before: Mastering the Habits of Our Everyday Lives

I have bad habits.
Really bad habits.

Not bad, as in selling dime bags or lifting protein bars from the local health food store, but still, for all my Type-A-ness, there are some areas that could be tweaked.

I work out.

I eat right.

I run a business from home, write, act, and seem to be in a happy-go-lucky mood daily. Everyone quips, "You are

64

so organized! How do you do it all?" Well, okay, I do have some pretty sound systems and plans in place to help keep me on track, but for all of those there are also several loose ends in my life.

Wanna take a peek?

• I've been sleeping on my naked mattress all week while my husband has been away because I'm too lazy to put on the mattress pad and a clean sheet.

• There is a pile of clothes on the chair in my bedroom. The chair I swore would not become a breeding ground for piles of clothes. I'm awful at putting things away.

• Put a basket of chips and a bowl of salsa on my table, and they are gone. Gone, I tell you. (The reason I may seem so over the top about my own nutrition—which, really, I'm not *that* over the top—is because I can binge with the best of them.)

"But wait!" you say. "Those are healthy!"

Not when you scarf down repeated servings complete with nuked cheese on top. Even too much healthy food is unhealthy.

• I'm a horrible cleaner. And I leave it to George. (Really, at this point we should just hire someone.)

• My Kindle Fire gets more use streaming Netflix than it does as an e-reader.

• When I do read (daily), I find myself in the middle of no less than four books at once.

• Speaking of books, I've renewed the same library books six times now. I've had to return them and then check them out on my kids' cards. I just haven't been able to get to them, but I don't want to give them up. Pitiful.

- I use my husband's razors. I'm too lazy to get my own.
- I stress-eat. Especially bags of chocolate chips.
- I've not worked out in four days. "Four days? So what?" you say. I'm a wellness coach. Exercise is what I do! Four days off is a slip at risk for becoming a slide.

"What?"

Yes, it is true. I'm off to Sin City on Wednesday and will be walking, walking, walking (mainly inside the MGM, which is grand), working out, working out, working out, and up by 5 a.m. each morning. So, yep. I took a few days off from exercising . . . which is one of the reasons I am completely stress-eating. Funny what happens when one doesn't exercise. The mind starts getting wonky. Crappy food starts looking like a great medication for the wonky mind. All lies. Shall we continue?

- I started writing this a few days ago. But then fell into a *If You Give a Mouse a Cookie* routine and became distracted by the mess on my desk, which led to more distractions. Squirrels! They are everywhere.
- I have baskets full of paid bills that need to be shredded or filed. I'm talking baskets . . . plural. I just asked a friend if I could borrow her shredder for the entire summer.
- I let my children watch movies with language. Yes, *that* type of language.
- I'm a horrible procrastinator. Even now, as I type, I am procrastinating. My goal for this morning: make the bedroom beautiful for my husband so that when he comes home tonight it doesn't look like we're living in a tenement with a mattress on the floor and a toilet in the corner. Okay,

there's no toilet in the corner, but really, I should make the bed.

- You can't even walk in my attic. It's like I opened the door, threw everything in there, and closed the door. Actually, it's not *like* that, I *did* open the door, throw things in, and then close the door.

- I seldom do my hair. I should buy stock in bandanas. This is always on my "bad habit" list.

- I have a habit of always having a "project." I see projects everywhere. Probably because, as I already mentioned, if you are paying close attention, I don't clean very well, and I procrastinate.

- Sometimes, if I work out in the morning, I don't shower until the evening. True story.

"Gross!"

You know what? This is no different than a mom of young children not getting a shower until later in the day. Relax. The problem? Or, rather, the situation? I work *and* work out at home. *Plus, they are one and the same.* If I smell, I'm sorry. I look good for church. And parties.

On a more serious note:

- I forget to send cards/gifts to those who have had babies, even my closest friends. I just forget.

- I'm horrible about knowing what to do when someone loses a family member. I tend to freeze up.

- I hibernate and withdraw when I've been hurt, or even slightly maimed. Like most people, I've been burned. This is my way of coping, until a true, biblical "Jonathan" lifts me out of my slump.

- There are no white lies. There are are only lies. I've told a few.

You wanted me to say that I've picked my nose.

Well, I have.

And so have you . . .

15
Don't mute yourself

When you pursue a calling, you will find a community of supporters to champion you along the way. It's not up to you where these people come from or even how to locate them.
— Jeff Goins, The Art of Work: A Proven Path to Discovering What You Were Meant to Do

It's not like I think I have anything particularly revolutionary or earth-shattering to say.

I really just make commentary about stuff I see/read/experience. At church. Online. In culture.

But perhaps, just perhaps, I'm viewed as *that* old lady sitting on her porch. And by *that*, I mean I'm conjuring up visions of Mrs. Dubose in *To Kill a Mockingbird*: "Don't you say 'hey' to me, you ugly girl!" Am I *that* lady? Only, here in this book?

I don't think so. There are way more opinionated busy-bodies than me out there. Some simply insert themselves into conversations and situations that don't even involve them; several gossip about this stuff to other people. Me, I write about it. At least you know where I stand, eh?

Being in network marketing (which is not a pyramid scheme—please do your homework) has opened my eyes to a lot. I've had to learn the art of adopting a stance of "I am not responsible for how so-and-so responds to my posts or information," as well as the all-too-difficult adage, "Don't take it personally," which is ultimately necessary if I am going to run a successful business. Why? Because often I do take it personally. I'm still learning.

What does this have to do with being a pastor's wife?

Everything.

This week, I was blessed to have conversations with two different people who both had the same "word" for me. These two women came to me independently of one another. They don't know each other. They are not local. Only one is a Beachbody Coach (lest one think I live only in that world), but I communicate with both often. Both women are believers. Both felt compelled to share a word with me that had been lingering on their hearts and minds for about a week.

Both messages were the same—communicated with different words, mind you, but the same.

"Don't mute yourself."

You've got to be kidding me.

But, I'm supposed to be kind! And gentle! And be friendly to everyone! And not rock any boats! And be careful! (Slight exaggeration here, but unless you've walked in my shoes, there is this unspoken pressure.)

If anyone needs a big red "mute" button, it's me. I blow it with my mouth and keyboard more often than not.

And yet, God has shoved me to share my passion to help people set goals and make real change in the multifaceted crevices of their lives. Long-term, feet to the pavement, sweat on the brow, "ouch, that wasn't pleasant, but indeed necessary" change. I tend to scoff at anything else.

(Oh boy, here she goes again.)

Relax. I just really wanted to find a place to use the word "scoff."

Personally, I used to phone it in. Excuse my language, but I was really good at giving a half-assed effort to many of my goals. And for that effort, I got a B in pretty much everything. See, I grew up being "pretty good," when just a bit more effort would have made my work remarkable. Do we need to be remarkable? Perfect? The best? No, not exactly.

(I feel a "but" coming on . . .)

However, if someone has even a hunch that they can be remarkable in a certain area, and they embody the goods to put forth that sacrifice and really do great work (and we have Christ . . . so yeah, we have some untapped power), and yet they willingly/willfully choose not to put forth the work to get 'er done, then, yes, I think that's pitiful. If I may be so frank.

"Sure."

Thanks, Frank.

Thankfully, I'm describing an old me. An old creation.

One that still creeps up from time to time, until I muzzle it, box it up, and send it packing.

I desire all of us to put forth the absolute best effort possible. In everything. "Best effort" meaning . . . well, *best* effort. To choose effort over ease. Challenge over convenience. Invincibility over immediacy. This doesn't mean that everyone will win the All-Around in life. And yet, everyone has been blessed with God-given talents and abilities in *some* area, as well as offered the chance to hone new skills. Listen, I dabbled in average for years. I was great at average.

Guess what? No one pays for average. Thank you very much, John C. Maxwell.

If a pipe bursts in my home, I don't call just any plumber. I want the best.

If my kid is having trouble in school, I'm not going to call the tutor that is just kind-of good at what they do. I want top of the line.

If I want a fantastic meal, I'll pay a little more for quality ingredients.

I invest.

We are all tempted to settle. Yes. Tempted.

My role/job as a Beachbody Coach has served me well in this area. I was forced to endure being uncomfortable. I had to communicate my goals publicly. My role as a coach seeped into other areas of my life that I had buried away in the basement. I now coach. And not just fitness and nutrition.

God placed me as a coach. He placed me in this town and at our church. He placed me in the lives of people all over the United States. It's crazy. But that's what's happening.

So, until further notice, from Him, my mute button is off.

You may want to cover your ears.

16
A trusted advisor doesn't blow sunshine

Take good counsel and accept correction—that's the way to live wisely and well. —Proverbs 19:20, The Message (MSG)

I can dish it out.

But can I take it?

It may surprise you to know that I actually ask for it. Often.

Advice. Feedback. Help. Notes. For a kick in the pants, even. From people who know me. And know me well. But don't misinterpret this as my simply seeking out those who love me so much that they won't dare tell me I'm doing something wrong. Though it's natural for us to seek out the confidence of those who will listen, empathize, and then give us a pat on the back and say, "It's okay" regardless of the situation . . .

It's not okay.

Nor is it the depth of friendship I desire.

As I get older, my circle tightens. It has tightened significantly over my four years living here as a small-town girl. I chalk it up to being the new family in town, who everyone is curious about in the beginning and wants to get to know. And then, after learning the muckity-muck and the flibbity-floo, those friendships fade into acquaintances. *That's not a complaint, as much as it is an observation.*

And then, you meet the "solids."

They are smaller in number, and rock stars in depth.

They listen to your stories—over and over—pretending they've never heard them before.

They celebrate your successes.

They give without expecting a return.

They tell you when you've goofed and when to put a sock in it.

They both call you . . . *and* they call you out.

They ask you tough questions.

When you hit snags, you unsnag, and move on.

Sometimes, I sense that church folk just want to make nicey-nice with each other. (What is up with the muckity-muck, flibbity-floo, and nicey-nice? Whatever. I'm on a roll.)

And by make nicey-nice, I mean, we're afraid of confrontation and conflict. We are fearful not of *having*, but rather, of *stating*, opposing opinions. And, we forget that speaking the truth in love is something we are called to do, which means checking in with a brother or sister in Christ when concerns arise . . . and no, doing so is not judgmental.

It's called friendship. Real friendship.

I have those people in my life. And I seek them out. Often. To check myself. They ask me uncomfortable questions. And guess what? They don't always agree with my answers. They aren't afraid to say, "Jo, back the truck up. That was uncool."

And then, we continue on, just as we have been.

Here's the kicker: many of those folks are not actually here.

And this can be hard for a pastor's wife. This can be hard for anyone. When you've lived twenty years in one city, and twenty years in another, you have a history—and a bond elsewhere. Upon moving to a new city you enter a story already in progress, so navigating your place and settling in to the plotline can be arduous at times. Maybe more so for me because I'm not a "let's just smooth it over" type, but more of a "hey, there's a bump—let's tackle it!" type of gal.

All this to say, I have my few close friends, only, not necessarily church members. (Gasp!) When you have a spouse on staff, sometimes you just gotta check-in elsewhere. So, I go to these few to ask if I'm crazy and because I trust they will tell me the truth about myself. And not the Osteen truth of "You can be everything God designed you to be!" (Buddy, if I could be everything God designed me to be, I would be perfect in *this* lifetime. Ain't gonna happen. I seriously suck at some stuff. Back to sound theology . . .) It's not human nature to respond all hunky dory upon hearing someone share that they are concerned about a decision we've made or how a situation has been handled. But to ignore friendships like these is to remain at the shallow end of the pool.

I'm thankful for these folks, and I know that, while setting me straight, they also won't jump ship.

My circle does not merely include those who blow sunshine and sweet nothings my way. Nope. They are the people with whom I can share my true intentions and deepest emotions, and with whom I can also receive critical feedback that can help with my spiritual/personal development.

And, they allow me to do the same for them. (And they *still* go to bat for me! What?)

I sincerely hope that all of us have at least a short list of those who can be trusted to stay the course through the fun, as well as the funky times.

Surrounded by yes–men (or women)?

Be mindful of that.

17
I'm that person

Discernment is God's call to intercession, never to faultfinding. —Corrie ten Boom

No need to duck.

I'm not slinging anything at you.

Sometimes I have a hard time knowing if I should tone it down a bit: my opinions, my personality, my leaning towards being outspoken.

And then, I'm reminded of the times God has either spoken to me directly in a dream (yes, à la Joseph style), or began moving my pen with abandon before hearing a sermon or a testimony, only to find that the spoken words matched the thoughts I had just written down.

There is some discernment going on. It's more than intuition. Some dreams are now long forgotten, but when they first occurred I obediently followed up with the person God had placed on my heart while I slumbered. Only one stands out in my mind now; others have faded away. What I do remember, however, is that upon addressing what I saw in the visions, I discovered the dreams to be spot on—not down to every tiny detail, but eerily true nonetheless.

Whether it was during my time as director of campus ministries at Trinity College, when I woke from a dream knowing that a particular student was contemplating suicide, or the confirmation I feel after I write a marathon post and am told by someone—strangers even—that the word was for them, there is something to this spiritual gift.

And, frankly, it's not always welcome. By others. Or myself, even. For I don't always use it well.

That's hard.

For the intention is for good.

Unfortunately, while helping is the goal, the perception can be: "Here she comes again . . . take cover."

The thing is, that doesn't stop me. To be silent would be direct disobedience. Sure, this often puts me in the hot seat, but to ignore the "words" would have me living a vanilla existence.

Instead, I call it out. Thankfully, I've learned to ask better questions, even though I rarely choose a middle-of-the-road stance. What does middle-of-the-road mean anyway? Safe? Because walking down the middle of the road is far from safe. Walk down the middle of the road and you have a greater chance of getting hit! Thank you kindly, but I'll choose a side. Here's where it gets tricky, and where I'm learning that approach is indeed important. Disagreement can be perceived as disrespect. (They are different.) Taking a side can perceived as rude. (They are different.) *How* you proceed in communicating beliefs and concerns does matter.

Discernment is not a popular gift. My thoughts are often black and white—not a lot of gray, except for the terrific shade of deep gray on my nails right now. Many don't enjoy hanging out with "those people." See, I don't play games very well, or dole out empty compliments, or strive to make everyone feel good all the time. I'm called to something more than that.

"Give them grace!"

I do. Maybe I have a wrong definition of grace, but I think the word can be misused when we are uncomfortable about addressing a concern with a friend. Grace, to me, is to love them unconditionally in the midst of a rough spot, not to avoid conflict or confrontation in those areas where they may be having difficulty. Choosing to not talk about that "something" isn't grace. Grace doesn't mean ignoring a problem and hoping it goes away because "it's not our business." Grace is loving within that business. Avoidance is simply . . . avoidance. I often wonder, what if I hadn't approached that student who I feared wanted to end their life, because it wasn't any of my business?

But, it's stuff like this that can leave a personality like mine lonely at times.

But don't worry! I'm okay! I actually like who God created me to me. I'm just sharing from my heart.

I surround myself with those who are not simply interested in surface-chatter. People who call me out when I sound judgmental or am gossiping. ("What? You gossip?"

Yep. Sure do. And chances are you do too, so relax.) The thing is, these are people who *know me*. And people who love God in ways I aspire to and respect. (And, I can have fun with those folks, too!)

Perhaps, perhaps, perhaps, it is this discernment that helped me go from teaching an acting class of four-year-olds to privately coaching some of the most talented youngsters (who are all grown up now) on the north shore of Chicago for ten years—and being fought over for my services. Why? Because I actually *coached*. I said the things that needed to be said, so that improvements could be made and those kids could clinch those roles. I didn't tell each private client they were brilliant. I told them when they were flat or needed to stand still and stop "acting."

Perhaps, it is this discernment that has quickly catapulted me to a top coach in Beachbody, where my clients are successful because I don't sugar-coat and tell them it's going to be easy. I'm not loose on pats on the back. And I certainly don't throw them an "it's okay," when they skip a workout. Nope, you asked for a coach. So, what's the obstacle? And how do we go over, under, around, or pick it up and hurl it? Many clients stay. Others choose to go.

And, yes, it is this discernment that will drive me to check in with someone who is most definitely avoiding me, to find out if there is some unspoken issue between us, or if I've heard talk of someone being upset with me, I'll go directly to them and ask, "Have I offended you in some way?"

And listen, I'm no saint. I've blown it just like every human out there. So I question myself. I over-reflect. I second-guess.

I'm *that* person.

And then, I put writing this chapter on hold in order to get on the phone with one of my coaches who is crippled by negative self-talk, to discuss "being transformed by the renewing of her mind." I launched into discipler mode immediately. We talked Scripture, focusing specifically on what she should be reading and listening to in order to evaporate the lies that reign in her head.

We connected.

We brainstormed.

I spoke bluntly.

We made a plan for change.

And suddenly, I'm once again back in my element.

Yep. I'm *that* person.

18
The lost art of the RSVP

Good manners reflect something from inside—an innate sense of consideration for others and respect for self.
—Emily Post

Disclaimer: Before you read this and think, "Sheesh, she sure does think she's all that!" know that I, too, have fallen prey to forgetting to RSVP. Remember, these are my confessions, *which means I'm not without guilt here. Okay, carry on.*

George came in the door at 7 p.m. I had expected him at 9 p.m., after teaching his class at church. I had adjusted my evening accordingly, which, sadly, meant no Girls' Night Out.

And then, in he walked. Surprise!

My response to his entrance was incredibly loving.

"What the hell are you doing here?" (Mind you, I had been going from 6:30 a.m. until 7 p.m., so I was a little ripe.)

"No one showed."

"Did you have any RSVPs?"

"No. Not for this class."

"Then why did you stay? Couldn't you have just come home at 5:30 since no one had RSVP'd?"

"Because often people don't RSVP and just show up."

Grrr, says the wife of the pastor.

"Honestly, I think if no one RSVPs, you should stick a sign on the door that says, 'No Class Due to No RSVPs.'"

"But what if someone shows up?"

Herein lies the deep difference in compassion that my husband and I hold for the lack of an RSVP. For me, if no one says they are coming . . . as in, no one replies in the affirmative, you don't hang around and wait. George, however, is wired differently. For him, someone who didn't RSVP may show at the last minute, so he should be available.

Perhaps that's why he's the one in full-time ministry. He is the gentle giant. I, *ahem,* am not.

It may sound like I'm harping on the church. Nah. This most recent example has more to do with accommodating a lack of response because one feels like they must (that is, the pastor). I understand George's compassion. I really do. I just don't share it after a long day; hence, these chapters are *confessions.* I do think we can all agree that RSVPs have become a lost art.

Today, I'm chatting about two different issues I have with the RSVP: my compassionate husband's response, and the lack of respect the RSVP receives in today's culture.

Let's review.

RSVP: *répondez s'il vous plaît* **("please reply")**

Often, we have to chase down RSVPs.

"Hey, I didn't get your RSVP. Are you able to make it?"

"Maybe."

Um . . .

"Did you get my invite? Are you coming?"

"I'll try."

Um . . .

Kind of need a yes or no here . . .

Some invitations come with instructions of "Regrets only, please." I like that. No need for me to respond. I'm headed to that baby shower and don't need to let them know. Woo hoo!

Let's break it down.

Responding to the RSVP, in whatever form it is requested, is simply following the directions as noted by the host or hostess, out of respect for their time and effort. After all, if no one can come, that will give them the freedom to make other plans.

We have telephones. Email. Facebook. Texting. There are several ways in which we can inform someone whether we are indeed attending or unable to attend.

Doing so is respectful. Not doing so is lazy. (Pot calling the kettle black, here.)

My personal example above is really a confession that I get frustrated when my spouse feels the need to stay late for an event, even though no one has RSVP'd that they are coming. (Don't worry, we'll work through that together.) Clearly though, George's RSVP for his class invitation meant for participants to reply in the affirmative if they were attending. So, in the future, if no one RSVPs, must he stay and wait? This is why many classes for which one must register (at community center, camps for kids, etc.) close down registration on a certain date and cancel the class if they don't have enough to fill it. Otherwise, an instructor may show up to teach or facilitate to the tune of zero participants. Not cool.

I am not trying to be the meany here. I just want my husband home if there is no class. Because, well, we kind of, sort of, love him being around.

So, how did the evening end?

With me sitting him down to enjoy the scrumptious dinner I had prepared?

Sadly, no. I texted my friend *stat* and found out where Girls' Night Out was happening, switched my reply to "yes," and hightailed it out of the house to where they were.

George was cool with that.

That scrumptious dinner that perhaps he had his heart set on?

It sent its regrets.

19

On coaches, cabbies, and skycaps

Among the things which we should regard as spiritual in this sense are our household or professional work, the social duties of our station, friendly visits, kind actions and small courtesies, and also necessary recreation of body and mind; so long as we link all these by intention with God and the great movement of his Will. —Evelyn Underhill, The Spiritual Life

L et's play "Find the Confession!"

It was an amazing five days in Dana Point, California.

I recently returned from the Leadership Retreat with my fellow Beachbody coaches. The retreat was chock full of useful information. What could have resulted in an overload of various ideas and systems that had no relationship to one another, ended up being a fruitful time of my needing to hear exactly *what* I needed for our team, *when* I needed to hear it, and in the presence of *whom* I needed to hear it. I attend events like these with the goal of bringing home tools to strengthen our team, only to end up taking tons of notes. Then, overwhelmed while sifting through all the interesting puzzle pieces, I discover the pieces don't actually connect into a valuable system for our personal team. It's the risk of "too many cooks."

This time, God gifted me with the opposite experience. After listening, taking notes, consulting with two top leaders, and having a major think-tank session with one of my coaches, we took the afternoon to discuss the new nuggets we'd learned, and used them to tweak our current system to assist our coaches and customers better!

There was an unspoken theme that kept knocking me on the noggin throughout the retreat. Coincidence?

Yeah. Right.

The theme led me to take a hard look in the mirror.

It was on Friday afternoon when a fellow coach alerted me to a time of prayer that would be happening in the morning with other coaches who were Christians. There was absolutely no way I wasn't going to attend. Sure, it was at 6 a.m., but if I could rise that early to write or read, or to get a front row seat to work out with Chalene Johnson, certainly I could rise early to meet and worship with coaches who also loved God and desired to serve Him with this Beachbody vehicle.

The same day I received the invitation, I was asked to answer a few questions on camera for the production team.

As I was asked the question, "What is the most important leadership quality of a Beachbody Coach?" the answer formed on my tongue and hurled itself at the camera.

"Servant leadership!"

"Can you actually restate the question and then share your answer?"

While I couldn't hold in my excitement, I did manage to compose myself enough to restate my answer.

"Without a doubt, the most important leadership quality a Beachbody Coach can possess is to be a servant leader to both our team and our customers."

It was a light bulb moment. All the notes I'd been taking up to this point were pointing me back to the core belief that I had to serve my team more intentionally. When that question had been asked of me, I realized, perhaps for the first time, what had to happen within me, so that my coaches and customers could be successful.

Prayer brought this idea even more to light. The Scripture and prayers offered that morning all revolved around the importance of service to others before self.

Following this, a brainstorming session with my teammate solidified how we needed to proceed.

Statements I've read in various leadership books, for both business and church, came to mind.

As the leader goes . . . so goes the team.

The speed of the leader is the speed of the pack.

I began to see that what I modeled would indeed affect the entire organization. Pressured much? No, not really. Freedom is what came out of this moment. That's what direction does.

As I hopped in the cab to leave, I felt confirmed, again, that Beachbody is my vehicle for ministry and healing in the lives of those with whom I have the pleasure of coming into contact, many of whom were once strangers. It was Sunday, and after five days, I was leaving this retreat with a new-ish plan for my team. The minor adjustments to our approach had been fashioned for us. I couldn't have come up with this myself.

God wasn't done with me.

My cabbie, Rami, who was originally from Nazareth, Israel, shared with us a bit about himself as we drove. A Christian, originally from Israel. Now living in Orange County, California, "which is hard, for so much is fake." We arrived at the airport after a wonderful thirty-minute chat. As we said goodbye, he placed a gift in my hands. Prayer beads made out of olive wood. "God bless you," he said. I hugged him.

Service.

Then, there was the skycap. The skycap who painstakingly took her time to weigh individual items from my suitcase to figure out what was causing my bag to exceed the fifty-pound limit. Ironically, it was all the gifts from the corporate office that put my bag over. She helped me identify them and remove them so that I didn't have to pay $75 in extra charges. And she did so with a spirit that convicted me. I wasn't a hassle. I wasn't a problem. I wasn't a bother. After taking her time to serve as she did, I glanced at her lanyard. It read, "I love Jesus."

"I love that," I said. "I knew there was something about you. I'm glad they let you wear it at work."

"I've been wearing it since 9/11. I've never been asked to remove it."

Service.

I am supposed to serve. My personal growth is nothing if I'm not leading my team and customers with an attitude of wanting them to accomplish their needs and goals.

And as for Rami, and the skycap? They were reminders to me to put feet on what I've learned. To walk in service, rather than just speak about serving.

This pastor's wife came home humbled. Looking in the mirror can be quite eye opening.

And that, if you've been searching for it, is the confession.

20
About that "day off"

Ruthlessly eliminate hurry from your life.
—Dallas Willard

This is a tough confession.

The day off.

Or, rather, the "kind of a day off."

Or, the "day off in theory, but never really a full day off."

Or, "Why does Dad have another meeting? It's Saturday."

You are going to have to trust that we certainly realize that part of the lack of taking a full day off each week rests in our hands. I mention this because my words could very easily be viewed as finger-pointing (something I have tried very hard to avoid in these confessions). And while I do have a few recommendations for churches in terms of self-care for their pastors, I also realize and accept that much of the responsibility to take a full Sabbath rest lies with us.

I can't control how each reader internalizes what I write, but with the disclaimers out of the way, "Once more unto the breach, dear friends, once more."

I am weary from my husband's seven-day work week.

Many pastors take Mondays off. But early on in my husband's career, we were advised not to go this course. Why? Because someday, when we had kids, they would be in school on Mondays, and if we wanted to protect a family day, we would need to adopt Saturday as that day. It was sound advice. And we've been fortunate to have been in two church positions that have allowed us to continue this.

Only . . .

- On some Saturdays there's a Bible study
- Or a church event
- Or a quick trip to visit someone in the hospital
- Or errands for potluck supplies
- Or an early morning coffee meeting—which won't take long

Very stealthy are these small fissures. We barely even realize they are happening, because really, they seem so slight. But they are cheeky buggers. Suddenly, that day off, which included a short meeting in the morning, turns into a half day, which winds up creeping into the evening hours. Now, we're fatigued from actually working, even though we weren't technically working, and the night is shot.

Again, maybe this sounds like complaining. After all, my husband chose to be a pastor, and thus, he should serve with joy. And, he does. But even pastors need time off. Even if only for one full day a week.

Seminary, however, doesn't teach Time Management 101 for Pastors (or, "self-management," which is a better description of what is needed, as coined by Chalene Johnson). Self-management is truly a learned and much-needed skill. If you don't have this skill down, the day off is used as catch-up. And trust me, cell phones don't help someone who feels the need to answer every text or call immediately. I would love to see seminaries offer a course on time management and personal business systems for ministry. Perhaps, just perhaps, a course like this would help with ministry burn-out. Or, perhaps churches should provide something like Franklin Covey training for their staff members. George and I have witnessed so many first-time pastors crumble in their debut positions. I truly believe this is an overlooked area of study for future ministers.

Another suggestion to help pastors protect their personal schedules (I'm veering off from the specificity of the "day off" here, but this is no less applicable) can be learned from doctors. In a group practice, there are on-call days for each physician, as well as an after-hours answering service. Perhaps some would find this too cold, and not personal enough to be implemented in a church setting, but what if—in an emergency—a church member called the answering service and was directed to the pastor on call? Isn't a ministry team like a medical group? Each pastor/director could take turns being on call on a rotating schedule. This way, someone would always be available for church members, but could also prepare for their scheduled on-call day ahead of time. This doesn't provide a complete solution for taking a day off, but it does provide a bit more consistency of scheduling, which, in my experience, has proven difficult for the majority of ministry professionals I know.

The most difficult part of the "non-day-off" syndrome (notice that I can't come up with a good hook phrase for this phenomenon) is just the ability and freedom to say, "I'm sorry. I am not available at such-and-such time or on such-and-such day," without requiring an explanation as to why. The pull to please is just too great. There is a fear of hurting feelings. Honestly, it's a boundary issue—for both parties.

Why this chapter?

This weekend, we took a two-hour drive to tour Frank Lloyd Wright's Fallingwater, then stopped at a roadside farmers market for pumpkin picking, visited Living Treasures animal park, hopped into a general store for penny candy, and then enjoyed dinner at a local restaurant. And that's where the conversation started. I won't even try to transcribe it perfectly, so I hope you'll be content with this paraphrase.

The kids: Today was the best day in a long time.

Us: Why? Fallingwater? The animals?

Them: No. I mean, yeah, those were cool.

Us: Then why?

Them: Because we were all together and Dad didn't have to go anywhere, you know, like to a quick meeting. (Zane hugs George for emphasis.)

I smiled at George, because had I given him my "I told you so" look, I think he would have cried. Thankfully, we were all in such a relaxed state that the comments didn't come across in an accusatory tone, and George was able to accept them with grace. Small actions over time create larger outcomes, for if the habit of protecting one's schedule is not happening during the week, then by golly, it most certainly won't happen when handed an entire chunk of a day. While we may recognize this as adults, it took the children speaking up for it to resonate.

Us: So, you both want more of this?

Them: Yes, when can we do this again?

I think it was the last question that really hit me. "When can we do this again?" Which seemed to imply that the next time we would be all together without interruption would take careful planning. My heart sank. We're not talking vacation here. We're talking one day each week.

My kids still love spending time together, just the four of us. I realize the clock is ticking to that point. We need to be better at protecting these moments.

But truth be told, pastors do feel bound to expectations of availability, because *they love serving*. And yet, serving must first begin in the home.

And when we say no, it's not that we are so busy. It's a desire to focus and use our days well, so that we have ample time for family moments like I described, as well as time to minister. It's a desire to be where we are when we are there, rather than to adopt a scattered, multitasking focus. We are not choosing one over another, but rather, learning to schedule effectively so that we do have time for both.

I'm not sure how to close this chapter other than to ask for some grace here as we recalibrate how to best use

CONFESSIONS OF A PASTOR'S WIFE

George's days off for the refreshment of our family. Because that one day did wonders for the four of us.

And experiencing days like that should not come once a quarter.

21
Stories from stage

What factors make you decide to take a particular role?
The actor always answers: "Because I'm afraid of it."
—Steven Pressfield, The War of Art

Whoa.

Worlds are colliding!

Confessions of a Pastor's Wife *and* Stories from Stage?

Yep.

Why?

Because of this.

"Mom, do you have to say any bad words on stage?"

Shoot. Here comes my Jiminy Cricket of an eight-year-old son.

"Well, as a matter of fact, I do have to say a bad word on stage. Just one."

"Oh." Obvious disappointment. "Is it the F-one?"

"No. They removed a few words from our script and that was one of them." I explained that we are doing this show as a charity event for women with breast cancer who need help at home, and that because of this, the audience would be a little different. Not your typical "theater crowd." Plus, due to the small town in which we live, thought is given to the script and how it could be received. Thus, the artistic staff adjusted it.

"But you still have to say a bad word?"

"Yep. The *s-h one*."

"Why?"

"Well, I'm playing a character when I say that word. A young, immature one. And the character would say that sort of thing. Honestly, I think it's worse when I use that word while driving."

"You say that word while driving?!"

"Um . . ."

"I heard you use the *a-word* while driving, but not the *s-one*."

"I said 'asinine.' I called the driver asinine."

"No, you just covered up what you really said with a fancy word."

Confession.

This pastor's wife will be using one piece of bad language in her next story on stage.

Is this an apology chapter?

Nope.

I'm simply letting you know, because some get all uncomfortable about that kind of stuff.

Don't.
I'll deal with my son's misgivings about it.
You deal with yours.
I'll let 'er rip.

22
Lessons in photos

Let Jesus doing the Jesusing. —Me

***The following essay came from seeing a photo of a Post-it note
with the words "F you fag. You are going to Hell" placed on an
anti-religion plastic car decal****. To the anonymous Post-it note
bomber, if you are real, then this letter is for you. If you have been
concocted by the actual photographer, you have only served to help
me birth a chapter on a subject I've been wanting to tackle for
some time, but up until now, had no muse. For I believe there is
a lesson here, regardless of whether this photo is true or a fake. I
was convicted enough by it, so my post stands.*

Dear Post-itangelist,
How clever you are! And so creative. Seems you've got
a unique ministry going on here. Truly, "out of the box."

I'm very moved that you have the desire to share Christ with strangers. Or, rather, with a stranger's car, from which you seem to have the astounding ability to glean so much about the owner. I often use a person's vehicle, clothing, and/or inanimate objects to form my picture of the person with whom I'm anonymously sharing Christ. Seems like you really have that down!

You used a really pretty color Post-it. I love green. It really pops against the black bumper. I don't normally carry around a pack of Post-it notes, but I'm glad you do, for it would seem to be a vital tool in your ministry. Much more effective than, say, actually talking with someone. (Don't forget to write those suckers off on your taxes!)

And if leaving an anonymous neon-colored note wasn't bold enough, you also went that extra mile when you went on to destroy something that was attached to the owner's car. With your bare hands. Wow! That *really* spoke to him. Putty in your super strong hands. You also timed your "sermon" really well! Ba-da-bing ba-da-boom! So stealth. Did anyone see you?

Someone did.

There's this guy named Jesus. I'm assuming you've heard of Him, because you referenced hell, which is in the Bible. Along with Jesus. Now, maybe I'm stretching, but seeing as you mentioned hell, I'm thinking you have, at the very least, an elementary knowledge of the Bible. You get an A+ for retaining the fire and brimstone part.

(By the way, while I realize you are a bonafide Post-itangelist, I do want to remove any pressure you may have erroneously placed upon yourself to confidently proclaim where a *perfect stranger* will be spending their eternity. It's actually not your job. You don't have to worry about filling God's shoes on stuff like that. Doesn't it feel good to have *that* monkey off your back? Phew! Glad I could help.)

Anyway, back to Jesus.

He saw you.

Rather, He saw your *heart*. (Which spurred your actions.)

Okay, let's not beat around the bush. He saw all of it.

But never you fear.

Grab your pad of ministerial Post-it notes. Scribble "Forgiven!" on the color of your choice.

Slap it on your forehead.

Grace.

Free for all.

23
On preferring solitude

I've begun to realize that you can listen to silence and learn from it. It has a quality and a dimension all its own. — Chaim Potok, The Chosen

I took Sunday morning off yesterday.

Not that I actually work on Sundays, so really, there is nothing formal from which to actually take off.

Call it a mental health day, or simply a desire for silence and solitude.

I just wanted to stay home.

And it wasn't because of the snow. Or the Polar Vortex.

No. I just wanted to be quiet. And alone. With God. His Word. And my books.

This happens more and more often these days.

I am easily distracted on Sunday mornings. Unfocused.

Unsettled. Craving silence. Solitude. Truly, my deepest insights, ideas, confessions, praise, a-ha light bulbs, and 2×4 what-was-I-thinking moments have not occurred sitting in the pew. Quite the opposite. I feel restless in a pew.

Do you watch *Sherlock*?

Picture when he's surveying the scene. About to solve a case. Words pop up everywhere. His head lights up with electronic maps and diagrams. The editing is frenetic. He seems to be gleaning information from every ounce of the location: words, actions, the minutest detail, down to a thread on a jacket. His senses are heightened.

That's me. On Sunday morning.

Not playing detective, no. For there is no case to be solved. But rather, unable to quiet the mind in the midst of people. I am an introvert, clothed in extroverted activities—coaching, acting, directing, public speaking—but really, I like my alone time. A lot. Had I the choice, all my Sundays would include rising early, a cup of coffee, my Bible, a devotional, God, and me. I don't have a lack of fellowship. I'm not a recluse.

What I do have is a lack of daily silence. And solitude.

There are times when I wish our services, from time to time, would simply consist of instrumental music and absolute silence. I'm not sure as a whole that we know how to "be." Without activity. Without constant stimuli, even in a church service. What would we do if we were just offered the opportunity to *be*? What would happen if we entered a church service to find no bulletin? No order of service. No announcements or videos, or worship band. No preaching. What if we were given some Scriptures and questions on which to meditate, and that was our hour of worship?

I believe we need this.

Not weekly, mind you.

But, it is indeed needed.

As I've mentioned before, Sunday mornings are not a Sabbath rest for me.

Enter: yesterday morning.

George understands. Had we to do it over, he would have two phones. A personal cell and a ministry cell. He recognizes that he is never completely "off the clock." Our day begins with his phone going off while he's still home. And ends with his phone going off. While he's back at home. I don't begrudge that. I do issue warnings about the boundaries between home and work. And the importance of creating spaces for both that do not collide.

Even ministers need to clock out. (I'm waiting for seminaries to offer classes on this. It is woefully ignored.)

And yet, I understand. The call to serve. To be available. To sacrifice.

However, even though I am not the minister, it leaves me craving what I've just described. Days without human interaction.

My response to the dings and chirps throughout the day is to go silent.

There is a toll that a minister's schedule takes on the spouse. I doubt it's recognized. There's no fault to those in the church, for it's just not something that is talked about or given much thought.

But if you see me bow out from time to time, this is why.

And, it's okay to ask. Really.

24
That's me under the
invisibility cloak

Watch out! Don't do your good deeds publicly, to be admired by others, for you will lose the reward from your Father in heaven. When you give to someone in need, don't do as the hypocrites do—blowing trumpets in the synagogues and streets to call attention to their acts of charity! I tell you the truth, they have received all the reward they will ever get. But when you give to someone in need, don't let your left hand know what your right hand is doing. Give your gifts in private, and your Father, who sees everything, will reward you. —Matthew 6:1-4, New Living Translation (NLT)

We are called to serve God, and support our husbands in their ministry. We are not *responsible for pleasing people—that includes church members.* —Quote from a wise friend

I had a very long overdue chat with a fellow pastor's wife this week. Two of them, actually. Each time I take time to do this, I breathe more freely because they reinforce statements like the one above. And they tell me I am not crazy.

Although I do have some "crazy" in me. We all do. Shh. Don't tell them.

But when it comes to personal experiences/observations/ outlook on church life, *which stem from my perspective as a pastor's wife,* it is comforting to know that, indeed, *I am not crazy.*

God, in His infinite wisdom, knows me like no one else ever has or will. (And that includes my husband.)

He knew long ago that my husband would serve Him in church ministry.

He also knew long ago that it would be best to keep me actively working outside the home, and, even, *outside the church.*

Some background.

There has never been a time in our marriage or his ministry when I have not worked, even once we had kids. And, perhaps not surprising if you know me, all my employment roles have had me in a teaching or coaching capacity: director/choreographer, director of campus ministries, acting teacher, music and movement teacher, private acting coach, and now? Fitness coach—which, really, simply has me discipling customers all over the U.S. in "lifestyle" fitness: spiritual, emotional, physical, etc. It's not all about the lean legs or the flat stomach. (Everything is linked. God knit us together so perfectly. All facets of our being are connected. We forget that. Emotions affect the physical and vice versa. You see where I'm headed.)

This is who I am. And one would *think* these skills would be used in an awesome way in church ministry.

However.

While I *have* served at church in the past (leading a high school small group, singing lead on the worship team, and serving in women's ministry for brief stints), I have only done so when I felt an honest-to-God *calling* to do so.

Not because it would look good. Or because I should. Or even because it's what Christians do. I have never taught children's Sunday school, unless you count the summer months at our former church where all parents were expected to volunteer on a Sunday, in order to give the regular teachers a break. And ... you do not want me in the nursery. Really. At any time during the year. I'll turn tummy-time into P90X-baby. Truly, unless I feel God tapping me on the heart and saying, "I'd like you to serve here," I don't. And won't.

For I've learned three valuable lessons.

1. Sometimes, feelings of obligation, and acting upon those feelings, come from a desire to please people rather than God. (Read carefully, I'm not talking about "calling," but rather, a feeling that I have to do this, in order to feel or be seen as "legit.") It's the trap of needing to prove oneself. Or, a lack of setting boundaries. And it can go too far.

Obligation with pure motives isn't dangerous. Obligation simply to please others is unhealthy.

2. I find ministry opportunities in my daily environment, and have been given many opportunities to share Christ outside church walls. I actually feel that this is where God uses me best for His glory.

3. Not all ministry is visible.

All three lessons lead to this: *Just because I'm not present, doesn't mean I'm not present.*

These days, my contribution is most often behind the scenes. My husband knows I support him, and we often refer to each other as a team. We also know that I don't need to show this by being at all his classes or church events. God knows my heart and my husband knows my heart. That's all that matters.

Other than a very public musical that I directed for the church (and, really, I was behind the scenes there also), you won't see me at many extra church activities. And while I'm present on Sunday, I'm in and out. I am close with a few people and enjoy getting together with my small group and in smaller gatherings. I am most definitely engaged in service opportunities, albeit behind closed doors, unseen, without recognition. No need to share details.

Fly-on-the-wall moment.

Just last week, God said to me, "Do this." His command was clear. It was specific. It would be a sacrifice. It would be weekly. It would stretch me. It would bless someone else.

I said yes, and immediately texted George to say, "Hey, God told me this, so we're doing it."

He knows how clearly I receive a "word" at times, so he simply answered with, "Cool."

Later, during small group we were asked to share something we could do for someone else that would be extraordinary. I love the idea. Without the sharing part. I explained to my group that God had recently asked me to do something that could be considered extraordinary, but I felt uncomfortable sharing the details. They understood.

My life as a Christian trumps my role or obligations as a pastor's wife, and thankfully, God has placed me in many other environments where I have opportunities to share Him and serve others.

So if your pastor's wife seems absent, know that we are there . . . just not always visible.

You never really understand a person until you consider things from his point of view… Until you climb inside of his skin and walk around in it. —Atticus Finch, To Kill a Mockingbird

𝒟𝒮

Depression (it's not about you)

Here are the two best prayers I know: "Help me, help me, help me" and "Thank you, thank you, thank you."
—Anne Lamott, Traveling Mercies

Why so many confession chapters?

Well, I give the readers what they want.

And according to my analytics, you, dear readers, like transparency.

Only, I'm torn in my response to the popularity.

On one hand:

• I hope that, as I provide an honest look into my life as a Christian, wife, mother, daughter, sister, writer, artist, and coach, the vulnerability, combined with a perseverance to overcome, begets more hope.

And then there's . . .

• Why are my most-read blog posts the ones outlining my difficulties and struggles? Are the readers thinking, "A-ha! See, she's not all that." (And not that I think, or am trying to be all that, but I sometimes wonder a tad if the reader isn't secretly taking joy in my hardships.)

Regardless, here I am not afraid to jump in the deep end.

Depression.

(There. I said it. Er, rather, typed it.)

I've been all about, "My husband struggles with depression," and "Winters are hard," and "I have a difficult time in the fall and winter," and "I bought a happy light!" That's so skirting around it.

Let's just name it.

Depression.

(I finally used the "D" word with George the other day. "Depressed"—following the pronoun "I" and "am.")

"I've been waiting for you to admit it." (He knew all along.)

It's why I hole up. Hibernate. Work out fiercely. Eat well. And sometimes binge. Write a lot. Invest my days pouring into my customers and coaches. Read Scripture. Read personal development. Say no to stuff. Avoid gatherings. Use essential oils. Sit in front of a happy light. Choose only positive relationships and activities that fuel me. Do not allow George to bring church "stuff" into the house. Focus on what's in front of me, rather than around me. Wake heavy. Am freezing—All. The. Time. I could lay in bed all day. Never get dressed. *Without some very deliberate and methodical habits in my life, I might never leave the house.* To some, I may be a bit obsessive and overly focused in certain personal areas.

There's a reason.

Survival.

During the winter, a doctor would put me on medication in a snap.

No thanks, Doc.

I will fight.

With every healthy decision I possibly can.

If you don't struggle with depression, you won't know. You won't understand. You may even take my behaviors personally. I know I did, when George first started dealing with depression. I would get annoyed. I would think he wasn't trying enough. And why couldn't he just adopt the "fake it, till you make it" approach to life? Cher's line from *Moonstruck* comes to mind: "Snap out of it!"

The thing is, we can't.

And that can be disappointing. For all parties involved. And while I'm highly functioning (because I would never want to give the impression that I struggle as deeply as I know many do), I may not function highly enough for the likes of others. I've had well-meaning friends ask me if I'm bitter about something because I don't linger at church on Sundays. I come, go to service, and leave.

Truth be told, I can hardly get myself out of bed on Sundays. And I crave quiet in the midst of this trial. The most uncomfortable place for me is the Coffee Not-Quite-an Hour, or just cheery hellos and "Happy Sundays!" Sorry. Those are situations I find very difficult to navigate. Often, I come to church simply out of obedience.

Depression.
(So there, I used the real word.)

I've had this for three years now, and it always arrives in late fall. However, this bully of a winter has exacerbated it. Thus, I realize that this year may have been worse than normal: more intense, and definitely situational. It totally blew the curve.

Last night I thought ahead to next winter and already started strategizing what I could do to not make it as bad as this winter.

The only answer I came up with was to move to a warmer climate.

And since that's not in the plans, I know I will have to face this head-on next year as well.

"Jo, if you didn't have your Beachbody community to get you outside, and your workout ethic, you would be in a pretty bad place."

My husband is clever, caring, and absolutely correct.

This pastor's wife cannot always be the initiator. She won't always be present. And, while I'm an actor, I just can't fake the smile or the conversation. If you see me online and wonder why I'm so present and positive there, and why I seem absolutely fine, it's because my blog and my online community are easier for me to connect with when I want to be physically alone. And part of why I am winning this battle is because of my commitment to share truth and strength with others who are in the same place. So you won't get mopey or crabby complaints, photos, or articles from me. As tough as it is, I am smart enough to know which road *not* to walk down.

Why feed my problem and possibly the problems of others? That would be irresponsible.

And there you have it.

How do you like them eggrolls, Mr. Goldstone?

$\mathscr{26}$
Mum's the word

Not my circus, not my monkeys. —Polish Proverb

Didn't George tell you?"

"Nope."

It's been a while since the chapter about my not actually being on staff at the church, and while I understand that people may not be aware that George doesn't share church member happenings with me, the fact is, he just doesn't.

Honestly, that should comfort you.

And it comforts me, for it forces George to leave work at work. And while some may take offense to being referred to as "work," truth be told, he works as a pastor, and as much as we love our church members, for us, when George walks in the door, church talk should cease.

It is not easy to refrain from talking about church. But I

learned a valuable lesson over the last two years that I can't ignore.

That lesson?

Button my lips and stay out of it.

Why?

1. Gossip: Yep. I fell smack dab face-first into gossip. No ifs, ands, or buts about it. I spoke when I shouldn't have, thinking that what I shared would not be repeated. And, those to whom I spoke, also spoke. See, therein lies the risk we take when we share information that needn't be shared. Only, it's never the middle man that takes the fall with gossip.

Nope.

It's the source. Thus, I have learned to shut it. Period. And because I don't always trust myself, this can keep me isolated from church members. I am that serious about not slipping into a conversation that I shouldn't be having. Been there. Done that. It sucked. No prizes won. Just a lot of grief.

2. Church life is stressful for a pastor's family: There's an underbelly to church life, that only a pastor, pastor's wife, staff, and elders and deacons know. And that stress doesn't escalate unless point 1 above kicks in. And sadly, we have a tendency to twist gossip into being "counsel" or "advice." But, even if that's curbed, what's a wife to do when her spouse is in the midst of church "stuff"?

In my opinion?

Refuse to let it in the house. While struggling with depression this winter, I placed George on a gag order. He was not to bring up anything going on at church that would cause us to gossip, or fill our home with tension. We had gotten into a bad habit of talking through things in the morning before work. And for us, this was detrimental and dangerous for our emotional states. Thus, I put the kibosh on conversations that were borderline gossip and absolutely emotionally draining. Just like a lawyer or accountant who brings work home, pastors can do the same thing. And truly, it's not always a healthy thing.

So, shhhh.

That's me. And there is plenty to be said about discretion in the ol' Bible, only . . .

You learn something when you get quiet.

It gets really quiet.

Not involving yourself in gossip can be an isolating decision.

But, truly, I'd rather be isolated than experience uncomfortable situations because I had diarrhea of the mouth.

Slow leaks are dangerous, and this pastor's wife doesn't want to be near a gossip pipeline, or allow toxic talk to fill up her house.

I choose quiet.

27
Holiday drama

We can't be won back with hipper worship bands, fancy coffee shops, or pastors who wear skinny jeans. We millennials have been advertised to our entire lives, so we can smell b.s. from a mile away. The church is the last place we want to be sold another product, the last place we want to be entertained. — Rachel Held Evans, Searching for Sunday: Loving, Leaving, and Finding the Church

How does this pastor's wife deal with holiday drama? Oooooh, you were hoping for D-rama. With a capital D.

Nope.

I'm not talking about that kind of Drama, the kind one finds in all families and congregations. Lord, have mercy. He, more than anyone, knows we all have enough of *that*

Drama. I don't need to be adding to it by spouting off some of the stuff I'd love to spout off about.

I'm talking drama—as in, church dramatic productions. A few things about me:

1. I am easily distracted.
2. I take strategic measures to stay highly focused.
3. At times, this could mean not talking to my family all day while I plan and regroup.
4. I am an extroverted, expressive, outgoing actress, who craves being alone and quiet.
5. I like quiet.
6. I spent much of my adult life hyper-focused on a career as a performer.
7. Did I mention that I like quiet?
8. Church is hard for me. (Because of the need-for-quiet thing.)
9. Two of my most memorable spiritual formation experiences included retreats that centered on HOURS of silence and solitude.

So, there's all that. (And no number 10.)

It's not hyperbole to say that every year I pray to be moved by Christmas and Easter. I mean, come on, these are the big ones in the life of the church calendar, right? And every year, my senses go into overload and I can't deal. I can't look. I can't hear. I can't sing. I. Just. Can't. I want to go sit in a monastery.

I'm treading very carefully here, knowing that inevitably, people will read what they want to read and hear what they want to hear from the words I am writing. People are just wired that way. But I've had a breakthrough in understanding myself and my relationship with God, and thus, here we go.

Let's talk church drama.

As in, dramatic productions. From my perspective. A perspective that isn't saying church dramas are right or wrong. Just sharing a confession of a pastor's wife who has a background in entertainment.

I directed a show at our church a few years back. It rocked. Literally. And yes, I'm patting myself and my cast and crew on the back for it. It was really good. However, it was not performed during a worship service. It was done as an optional evening out at the theater. For many, it was a worship experience. And I'm glad. Me, however? I was exhausted for months after we closed that show. High as a kite . . . and completely depleted. That's how I do theater. All in. I didn't even go near the stage for an entire year after that experience.

Now, bring that type of theater to a worship service and I get completely lost.

Not lost in worship. But rather, lost in the "production." The details. I've never been able to come to a comfortable place with the intermingling of worship and performance.

Why?

• I feel uncomfortable watching people play Jesus. It's a role that just can't be played. It always seems forced to me.

• I watch most theater through either a director or actor's lens. That doesn't mean I'm critical (in a negative sense). It means I watch from a performance perspective, and thus, when drama is done in church, all bets are off that I will be focusing on God in any way because . . . well, that bench just got tipped over, oops, there goes a mic, or wow, what a voice!

- Drama during worship takes me out of the quiet, inward place of worship I so desperately need in order to connect with the Lord, and plops me into a theater, as an audience member, where I do not want to be during worship.

Trust me. I have tried and tried to change this. Ask my husband. I have never been able to reconcile this for myself. And maybe, I'm not supposed to do so.

Enter: holidays.

There are sets. New music. Drama is coming. I sense it. I feel it. I'm almost scared of it. I know, it sounds paranoid and ridiculous. It's hard enough being a pastor's wife during the holidays without the added measure of being one who has been a performer all her life.

It is during the holidays that I want to run to a liturgically driven church and get lost in Jesus, rather than lost in whether someone's waist wrapping might fall off, creating a holy wardrobe malfunction. (I swear, I worry about this every Easter.)

This whole chapter sounds like a bad date with church. I hate to sound cliché, but let me say in all honesty:

"Church, it's not you. It's me."

I applaud creative efforts. I love thinking out of the box.

Only, when one possesses a distracted mind, tends to already live an overstimulated existence, performs impromptu musicals in the kitchen, and is often most comfortable in life when on stage, the senses yearn for the opposite upon entering God's presence.

To all who are about to get your worship on for Good Friday and Easter by performing in church productions, I am thankful for you. Truly. It's nice to see the arts brought to church, and it does indeed allow many to "see" the Scriptures for the first time.

I must confess, however, that God seems have other plans for how He initiates His relationship with me.

And . . . *scene*.

28
A year of loss

The Lord's lovingkindnesses indeed never cease,
For His compassions never fail.
They are new every morning;
Great is Your faithfulness.
—Lamentations 3:22-23, New American Standard
Bible (NASB)

That awful year. I remember it well. I recall directing it to take its exit.

No curtain call. No standing ovation. Just leave the theater and get the lights on your way out, if you don't mind.

Before I begin, let me preface this post by sharing that my heart is full of Love, Joy, Peace, and Hope. Capitalized, of course, for Jesus is Love, Joy, Peace, and Hope. So what may seem like a broken, downtrodden, and despair-ridden chapter, while revealing honest feelings, does not fully embody my overall outlook on life. The year may have served up some heartbreak, but even that cannot overshadow the truth of Christ's glorious presence in my life. Regardless of all that occurred this year, I have been changed. For the better. And I am entering this new year with abundant gratitude for being walked through the desert.

One has to recognize the desert to persevere through it. My personal deserts were marked by:

Loss of self: I homeschooled this year. And while it was a terrific experience, it was also marked by loneliness. Not a lot of adult interaction. When I began, I couldn't have known that the winter would also prove to rough me up emotionally. I all but disappeared.

I was glad to have Zane home, for he is gentle, loving, and a downright snuggly soul. I needed him. Without him, I'm not sure I would have gotten out of bed. I often wonder if one of the reasons God called me to homeschool was because He knew I'd need someone else home during the day from January to March. A beautiful result of our experience was getting to know Zane without his sister present, which doesn't always happen with child #2. Our relationship is better for it. The loneliness and frigid temperatures may have been heavy-handed, but we made it.

Loss of friendship: Phew. If the winter blues weren't hard enough, this was a year of friendships gone awry. But, as mentioned, God is with us in our deepest loss, and throughout the year, in the midst of my grief, He began to reveal my "lifers."

Loss of voice: I experienced silence this year. God taught me the value and sacrifice of discretion. As someone who has learned tough lessons from having an overly active tongue—especially when I didn't have all the facts—I now learned that one's silence can be just as equally misinterpreted.

Loss of life: A gal from my high school days passed away from cardiac arrest after a hornet sting. My dear Nanny left us a week before Thanksgiving. My precious neighbor, who made everyone feel like the most important person in the room, and will always remain a model and mentor in my life, lost a tremendously courageous fight with cancer.

But here's what happens when someone experiences loss. They start anew.

I'm big on "His mercies are new every morning," and I have a watchful eye on how God seems to be refashioning me. As my father once told me after I missed reaching a goal I'd worked very hard to hit, "Look back and see what you can adjust moving forward, *but don't linger there.*"

And thus, I'm not.

This is my farewell to that on which I've been lingering.

Enough of that.

No more lingering.

Clang those pots and pans! It's a new year!

29
Hanging up the hat

For everything there is a season, and a time for every matter under heaven. —Ecclesiastes 3:1, English Standard Version (ESV)

It's been a month.

A full month since my husband left his position as an associate pastor in congregational ministry, after serving in the local church for sixteen years.

People have asked:

"How do you feel no longer being a pastor's wife?"

Well, for one, I'm certainly enjoying not being called a "counselor's wife."

I kid.

Kind of. Although it is a relief not to be attached to my husband's position.

But while these reflections have primarily been about my experiences as one whose husband is in professional church ministry, this chapter cannot possibly be about me.

So, in answer to the how-do-I-feel question?

I am absolutely elated for my husband. He has found and answered a new calling. Even though that means:

- Giving up a full-time salary and benefits.
- Learning to build his own practice.
- Returning to school for yet a second master's degree.
- Answering (you gotta know this happens) so many questions about why he took a new position. (Many of these are weighted investigative questions, insinuating there is more to the story.)
- Serving in lay ministry at a new church.

What has this meant for our family?

Breathing room.

When someone is pondering a change, but, for the sake of professionalism, is understandably quiet about contemplating a new direction (except during discussions within the walls of one's own home), it creates a bubble. We had just been through a year where we learned the absolute value of discretion, and now we were having to practice what we learned as we talked, debated, and prayed, over a number a months, about George's next step.

He knew a next step was waiting. Lingering. Waving him over.

We didn't know the exact who, what, where, when, why, or how of this step.

We did know that he greatly values reconciliation within

relationships and has personal experience with the delicate dance of mental health.

I recall saying years ago, "The Lord will use your pain in the lives of others. Someday. Somehow."

Then, one day it hit us.

This guy should totally be a counselor.

And now, in his new ministry, he is one.

A new Sunday

Sunday looks a lot different for us now.

Come to think of it, Saturday does also.

During the week, George sets his own schedule. He doesn't rush out in the morning, comes home for lunch, works in tandem with me throughout the day with the house and kids, is learning new freelancing skills, and is truly more available, both physically and emotionally. Just yesterday, our daughter returned home from school to find him in the living room. She lit up upon seeing him.

"Cool! You are home!"

But Sunday mornings have been the most significant change for all of us. While it took the children time to adapt to a new church, and it will continue to take open minds as Sunday school and youth group begin, we all agree: we've needed this.

We hear the church bell ring. This is our cue to head out the door. Together.

We sit together. We rise together. We worship together.

We head out to lunch (one Sunday a month) or to the local grocery store to pick up an item or two following the service. We walk home.

Together.

As George desires to help individuals, couples, and families see the beauty of "together," his new position has revealed that *we* also needed more together.

That is my final confession.

From this former pastor's wife,
Be.
Together.

Epilogue
Where are we now?

I sit in the early service at church, conveniently hidden in the back of the sanctuary. This particular service is done without much amplification. The music is simple. The crowd is smaller. Usually, I walk to this service with my son, and then promptly walk home when it's over. It is then that my husband walks to church where he is helping out in a limited capacity. No longer a full-time pastor, he is busy with his counseling practice, doing a bit of pastoral care, preaching on occasion, and teaching Sunday school when needed, all while securing a second master's degree.

It's an existence not unlike the one we lived before he secured that first full-time ministry position back in 1999. A season in our lives where we pieced several jobs together in order to make ends meet.

One might find our situation stressful.

Aside from a few spontaneous and short-lived freak-outs, we are enjoying this season; resting in God's financial provisions as well as watching Him use my husband's gifts to their fullest potential.

Me?

Truth be told, church still leaves me a bit skittish.

Thus, I worship quietly, in the back of the sanctuary.

And that's okay right now.

I delight in the simple.

I delight in watching my husband flourish where he is currently planted.

Just as he has always done for me.

Confession: This former pastor's wife is enjoying being a "former," but I will be obedient if God places me in that role again.

Only, if that happens, you should know . . . I won't change a darn thing.

Acknowledgments

Mom and Dad, look how I moved the drama from the stage to the page! And to think, if I hadn't been the dramatic middle child, this never would have happened. You taught me to project, slow down, listen, and not quit. Which I didn't understand until I turned forty. Sorry it took so long! Love you both.

Mama A and Big Daddy, you've taught me that loving unconditionally and being gracious is truly not very difficult. I have been your daughter since I fell in love with that son of yours. Much love and respect for two people who have always loved me for being me. Quirks and all.

Martha, I trust you are singing loudly up there. No doubt, you are. You possessed a gift for helping me believe I was a valuable, creative person . . . of sound mind, even!

All while casually sitting and chatting in your kitchen. You contributed to my bravery. Until we meet again . . .

Liz, Katie, Angie, and Alyssa, the wise counsel you have given me over the years provided much-needed stability while wandering a desert. You listened. You advised. You supported. You loved. Thank you, ladies.

Cafe Kolache has served as the office where my coaching and writing businesses were launched seven years ago! Many of these essays were actually written in this home away from home, at the window table I claimed as my own. Kristi and Hugh, I knew when I first visited the cafe years ago that it would be my happy place. You have provided a community, where, not unlike Cheers, "everybody knows your name." Thank you.

About the Author

Joline Pinto Atkins, never shy about sharing her opinion about anything, even if not asked (this can be a problem), has been blogging for years on her personal site, TheCuppaJo.com. This certified Wellness Coach and fitness instructor also uses her weekly *Beaver County Times* column, "Shape Up with Jo," and web series, "For the Health of It," to preach the importance of living a fit life: physically, spiritually, emotionally, mentally, and relationally. Her passion is to coach others toward making adjustments and changes that will have long-term benefits for their overall health.

She has blogged in the past for the Pittsburgh Mom blog through the Pittsburgh *Post-Gazette* and the devotional site Daily Fast Fuel. Joline loves to tackle creative challenges, both behind the computer and for a live audience. With a background in theater performance and directing, Joline was honored as Outstanding Lead Actress in the 2011 season for the Pittsburgh New Works Festival for her role in the world premiere of *Pump* and continues to act and direct when time permits and whimsy hits.

She and her husband, a counselor, live outside Pittsburgh with their two children, both named after authors, and two beagles, who drive her crazy, but she'll keep them. (The dogs! The dogs! She means the dogs. Sheesh!)

Made in the USA
Middletown, DE
31 August 2019